Vocal/Piano

ISBN 978-1-61780-364-2

HAL•LEONARD®
CORPORATION

7777 W. BLUEMOUND RD. P.O. BOX 13819 MILWAUKEE, WI 53213

Visit Hal Leonard Online at
www.halleonard.com

COME FLY WITH ME

Words by SAMMY CAHN
Music by JAMES VAN HEUSEN

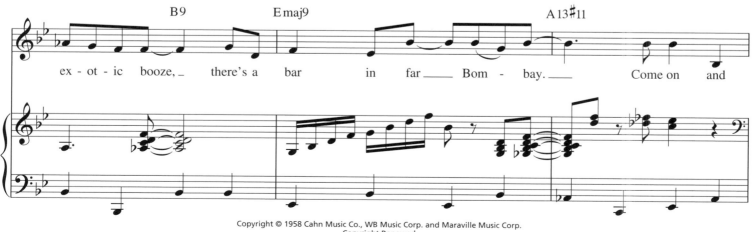

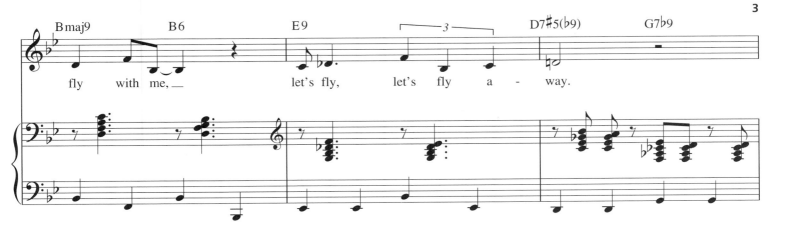

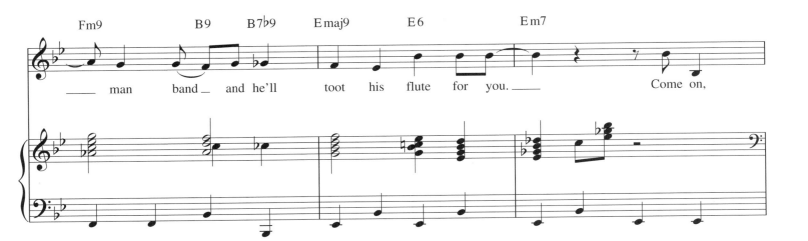

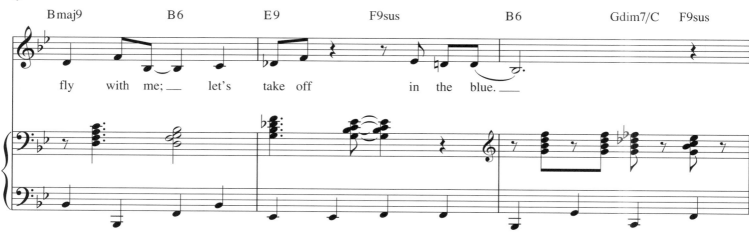

up there,

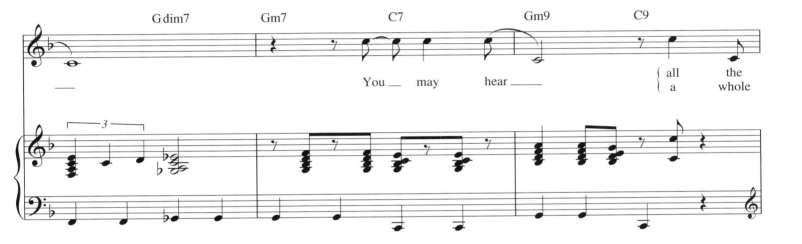

I'll __ be hold-ing you _____ so near.

You __ may hear _____ { all the / a whole

an - gels cheer be - cause _____ } we're to - geth - er.
gang of cheers just be - cause }

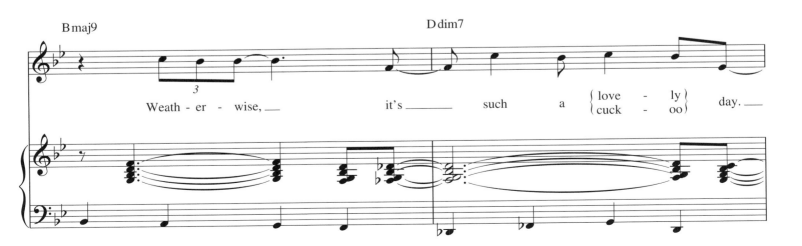

Weath - er - wise, ___ it's ___ such a { love - ly } day. ___
{ cuck - oo }

6

Cm7 ... F13 ... B♭maj9 ... B♭6

Just say the words _ and we'll _

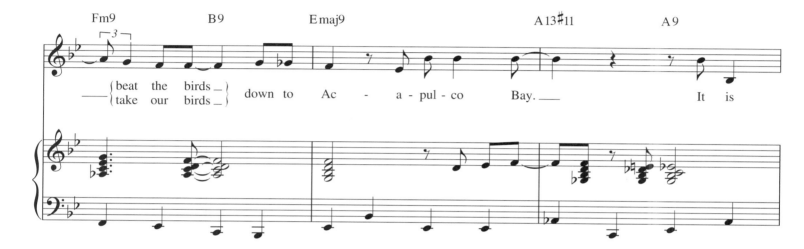

Fm9 ... B♭9 ... E♭maj9 ... A13♯11 ... A♭9

{ beat the birds _ }
{ take our birds _ } down to Ac - a - pul - co Bay. _ It is

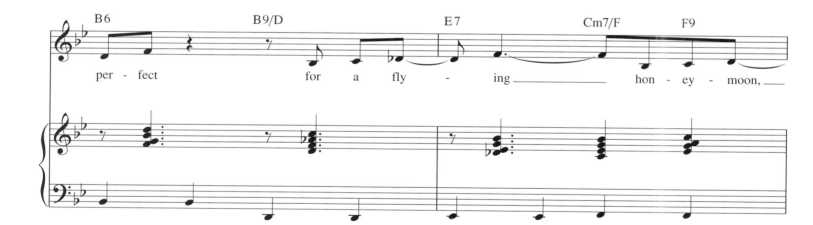

B♭6 ... B♭9/D ... E♭7 ... Cm7/F ... F9

per - fect for a fly - ing _ hon - ey - moon, _

B♭maj9 ... F9/A ... A♭6 ... G7♭9 ... **To Coda** ⊕ ... C9

{ they say. _ }
{ oh, babe. _ }

Come fly _ with me, _ let's fly, _
Come fly _

let's __ fly a - way. ___

AIN'T THAT A KICK IN THE HEAD

Words by SAMMY CAHN
Music by JAMES VAN HEUSEN

The room ___ was com-plete - ly black; ___ I

hugged her, and ___ she hugged back. ___ Like the sail - or said, quote,

"Ain't that a hole ___ in the boat!" ___ My head ___ keeps ___

___ spin - ning. ___ I ___ go to sleep and keep grin - ning. ___ If ___

this is just the be - gin - ning, __ my life is gon - na be

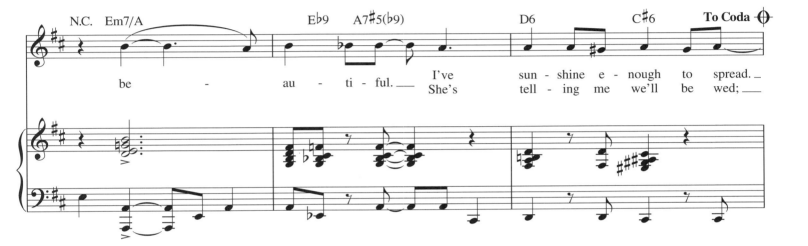

be - au - ti - ful. __ I've sun - shine e - nough to spread. __
She's tell - ing me we'll be wed; __

It's just __ like the __ fel - la said, __ "Tell me quick, __

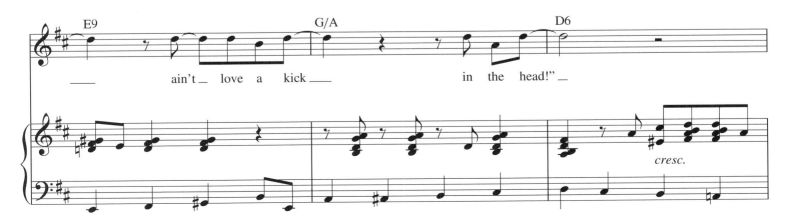

__ ain't __ love a kick __ in the head!" __

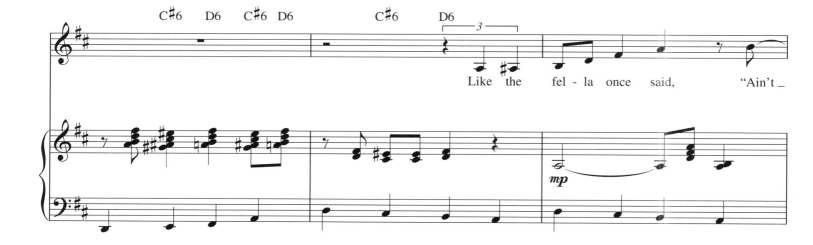

Like the fel - la once said, "Ain't

that a kick in the head!"

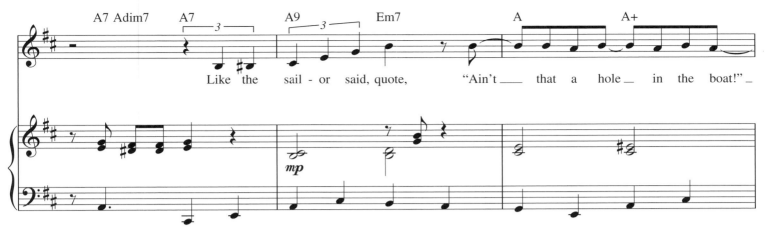

Like the sail-or said, quote, "Ain't ___ that a hole ___ in the boat!" ___

D.S. al Coda

My head keeps ___

CODA

she's picked out a king - size

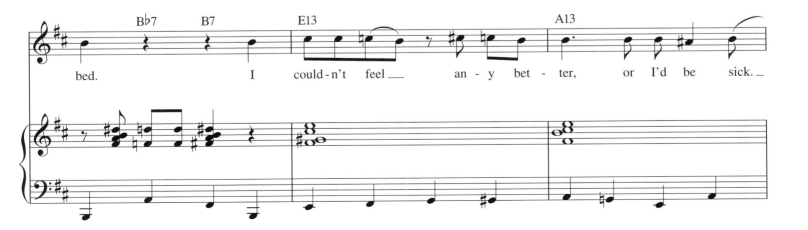

bed. I could-n't feel ___ an - y bet - ter, or I'd be sick. ___

Too Close for Comfort

from the Musical MR. WONDERFUL

Words and Music by JERRY BOCK,
LARRY HOLOFCENER and GEORGE WEISS

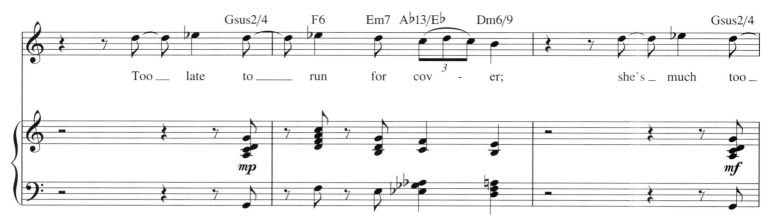

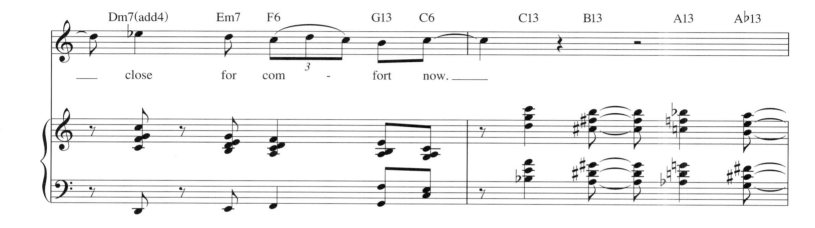

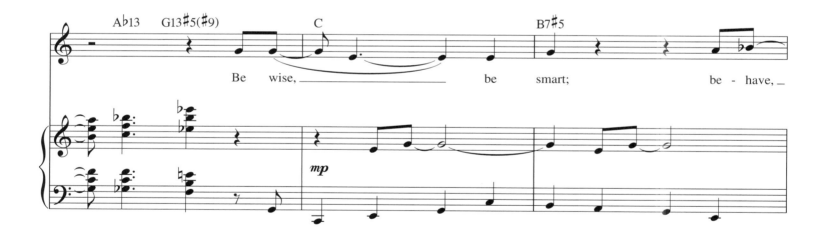

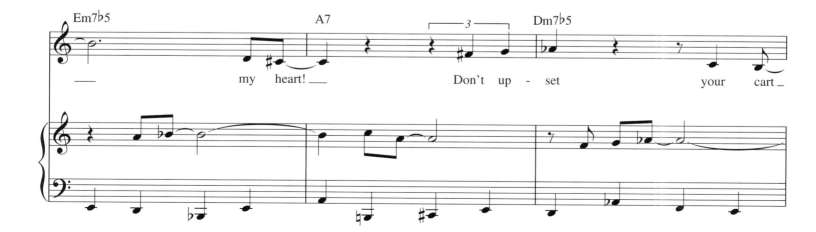

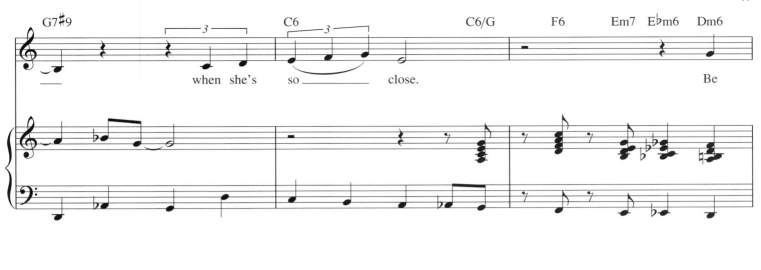

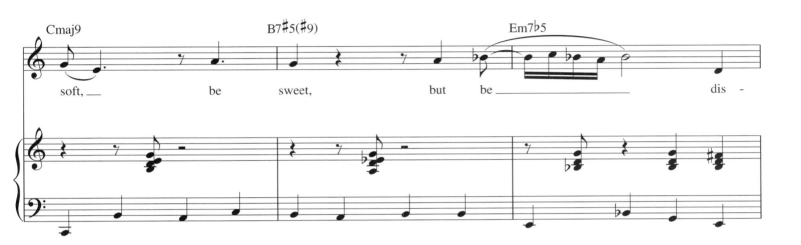

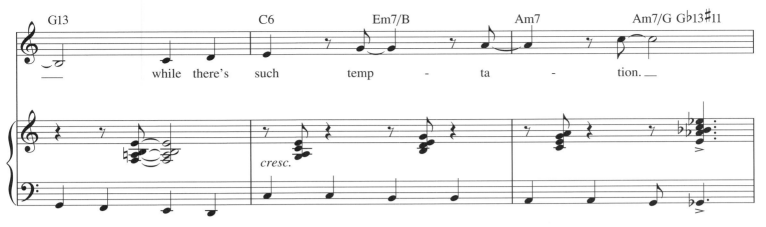

while there's such temp - ta - tion. ___

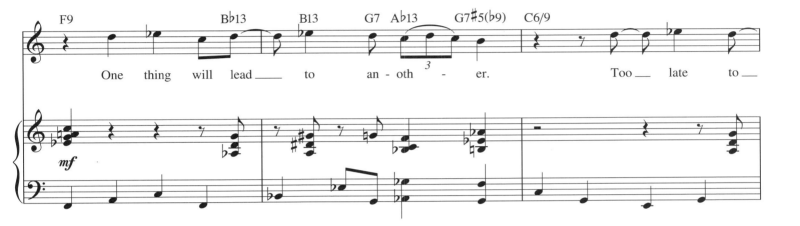

One thing will lead ___ to an - oth - er. Too ___ late to ___

___ run for cov - er; she's ___ much too ___ close for com - fort now. ___

Instrumental solo

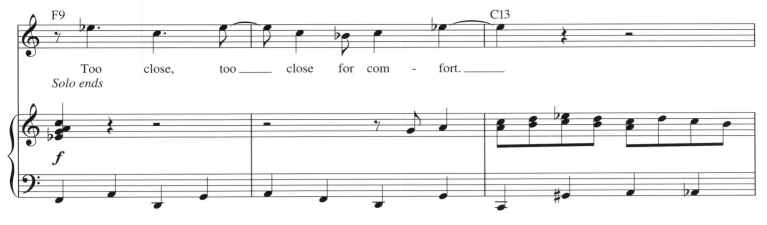

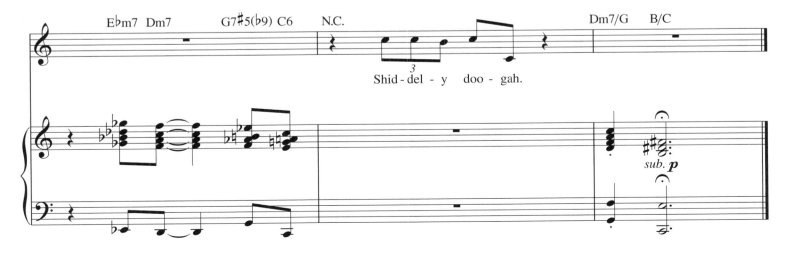

I'VE GOT YOU UNDER MY SKIN

Words and Music by
COLE PORTER

Moderate Swing

heart of ___ me, ___ so deep ___ in my ___ heart a-

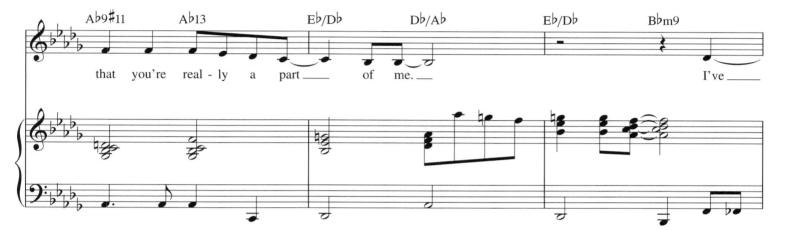

that you're real-ly a part ___ of me. ___ I've ___

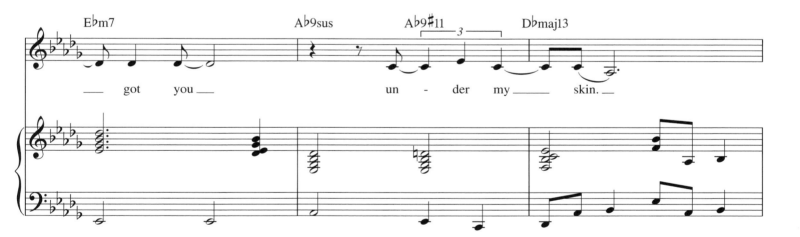

___ got you ___ un - der my ___ skin. ___

I tried so ___ not to give in. ___
(Instrumental on D.S.)

I've said ____ to my-self, _ "This af - fair, _

____ it nev - er will go ____ so well." _ A - but, a -

why should I try to re - sist ____ when, ba - by, I know damn _ well ____ that I've

got you ____ un - der my skin. ____ I'd

(Vocal ad lib. re-enters on D.S.)

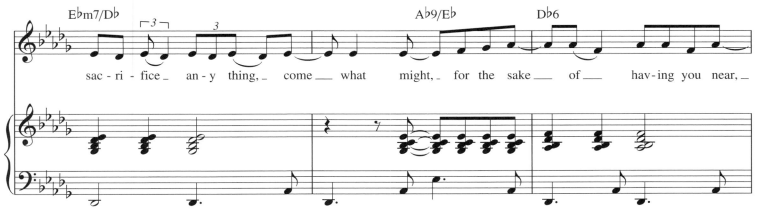

sac-ri-fice __ an-y thing, __ come __ what might, __ for the sake __ of __ hav-ing you near, __

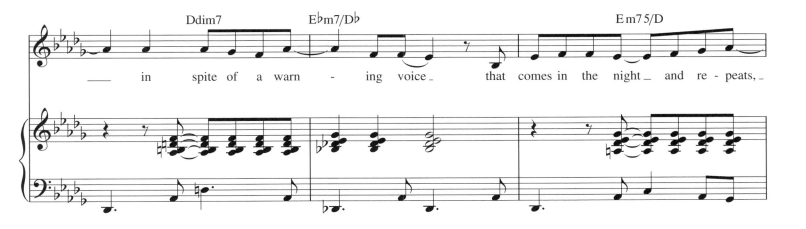

__ in spite of a warn - ing voice __ that comes in the night __ and re - peats, __

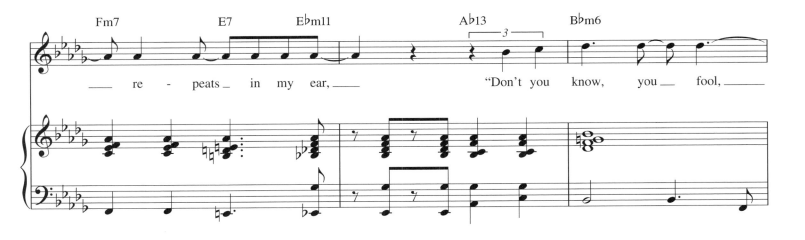

__ re - peats __ in my ear, __ "Don't you know, you __ fool, __

__ you nev-er can win. __ Use __ your men - tal - i - ty;

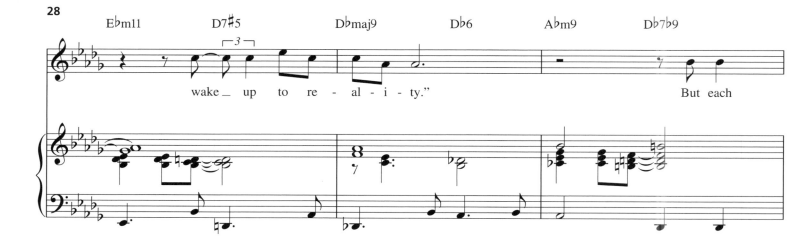

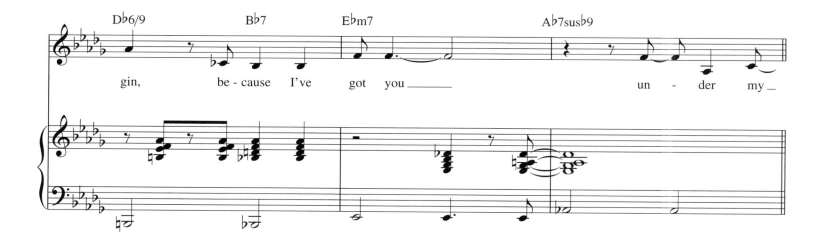

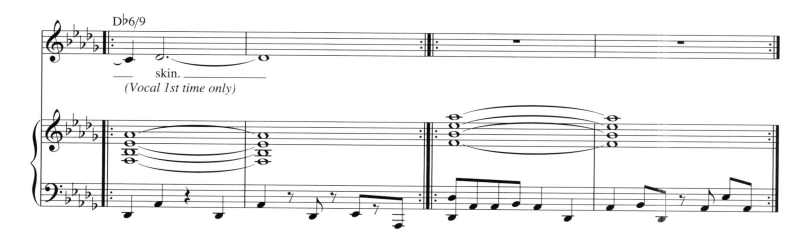

D.S. al Coda

stop just be - fore I be - gin, be - cause I've got you ___

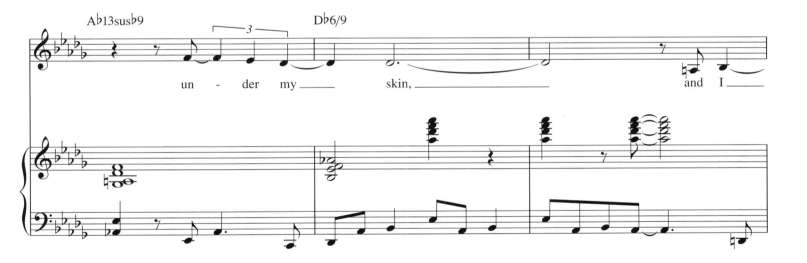

un - der my ___ skin, ___ and I ___

___ like you un - der my skin.

WHO'S GOT THE ACTION?

Words and Music by GEORGE DUNING
and JACK BROOKS

Moderately fast Swing (♩ = 180)

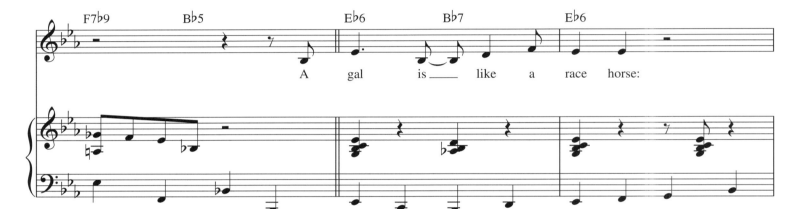

A gal is ___ like a race horse:

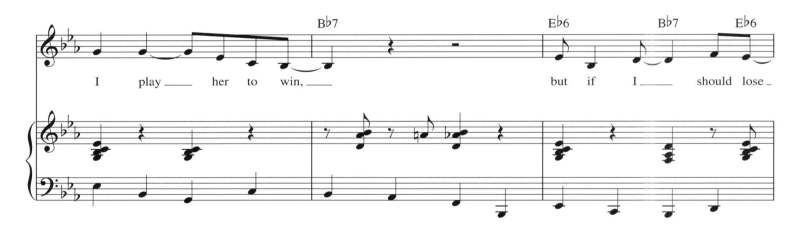

I play ___ her to win, ___ but if I ___ should lose ___

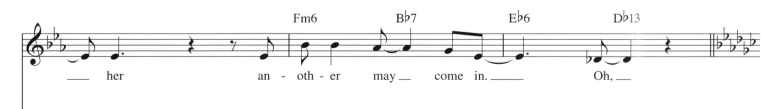

___ her an - oth - er may ___ come in. ___ Oh, ___

love can __ be like heav - en; love can __ be a joke. __

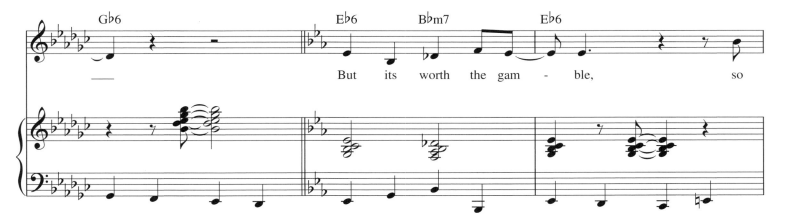

__ But its worth the gam - ble, so

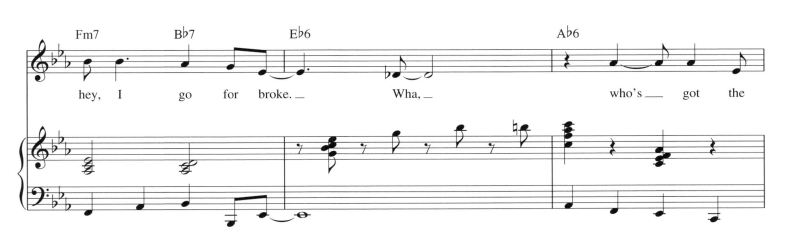

hey, I go for broke. __ Wha, __ who's __ got the

ac - tion? Who'll take a chance __ on love? Who's __ got a

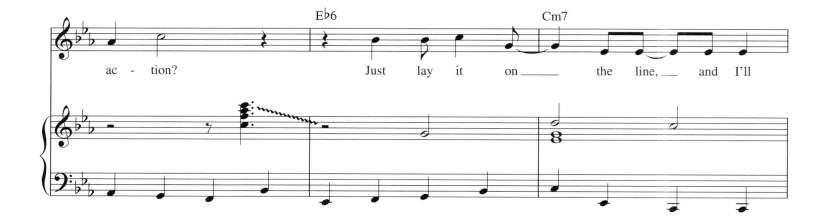

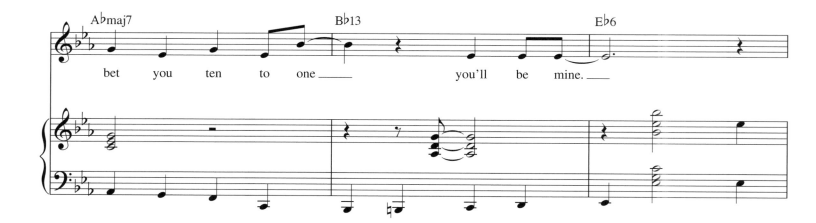

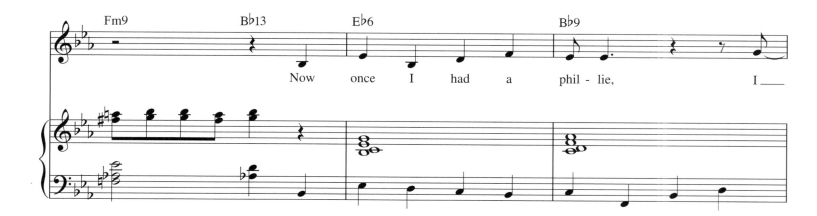

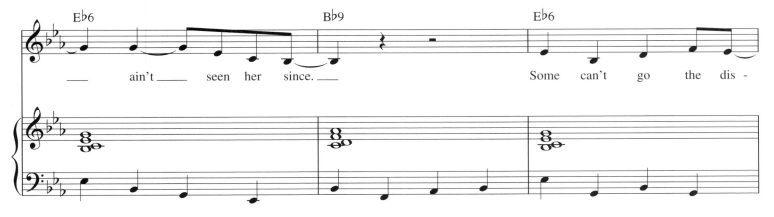

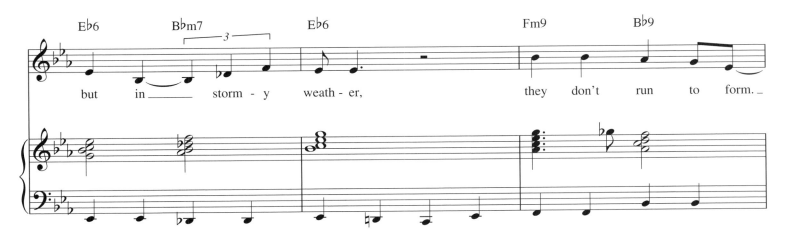

Aww, who's ___ got the ac - tion?

Who'll take a chance ___ on love? Who's ___ got a

kiss for me? ___ Give me one, and you get back three.

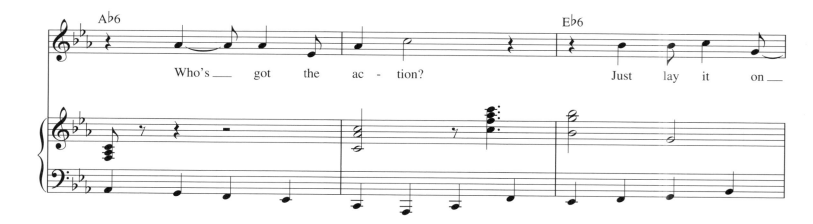

Who's ___ got the ac - tion? Just lay it on ___

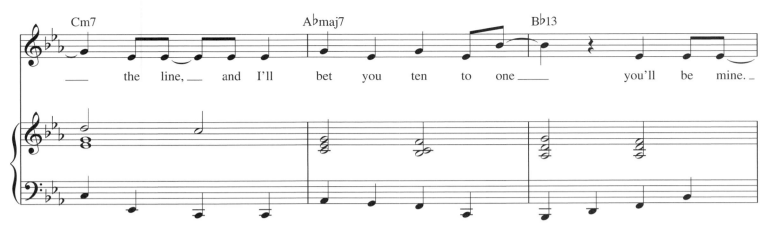

the line, ___ and I'll bet you ten to one ___ you'll be mine. __

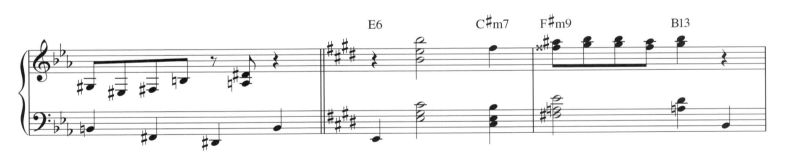

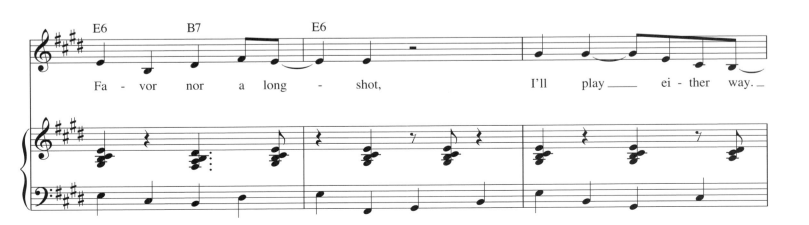

Fa - vor nor a long - shot, I'll play ___ ei - ther way. __

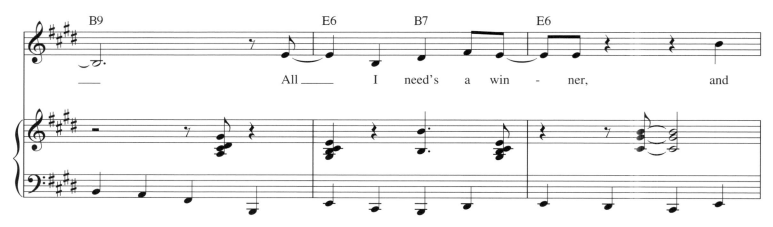

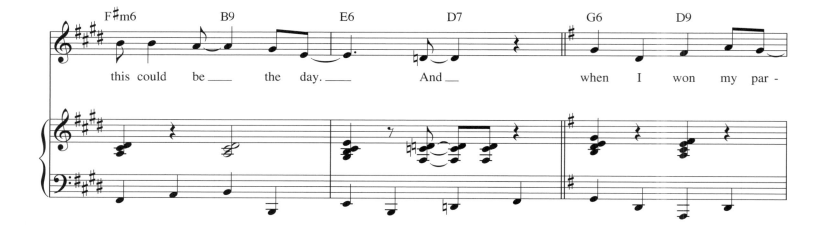

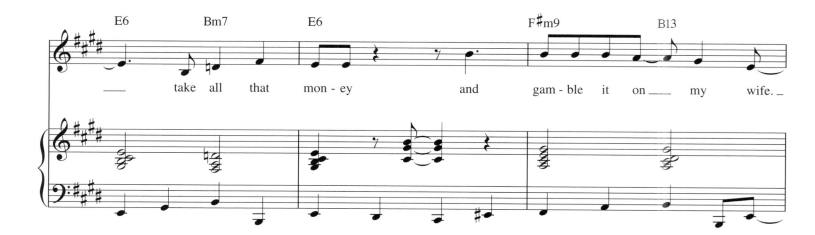

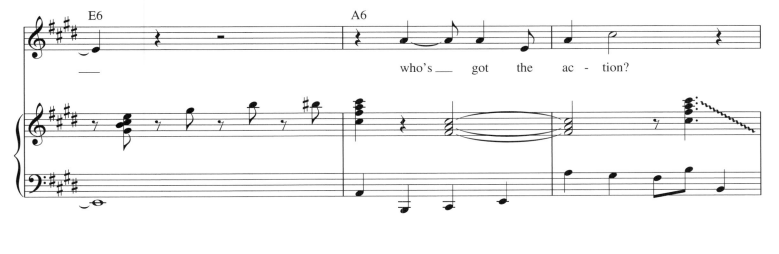

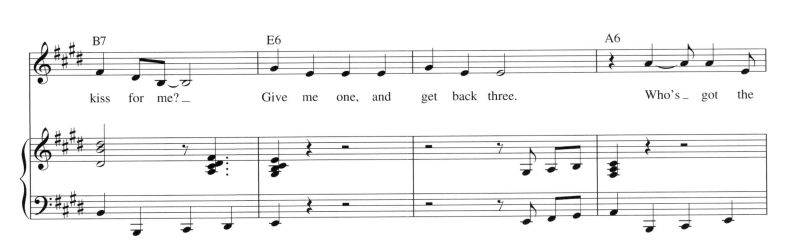

bet you ten to one, ____ bet you ten to one, __

____ bet you ten to one ____ you

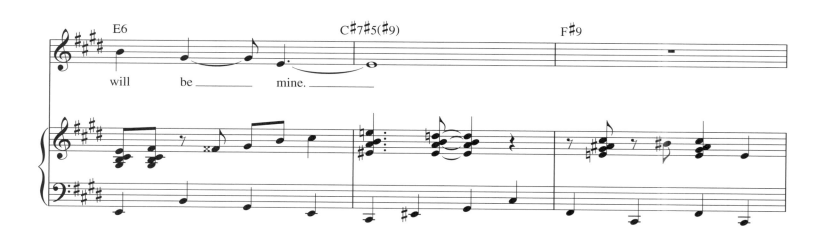

will be _____ mine. _____

A LOT OF LIVIN' TO DO
from BYE BYE BIRDIE

Lyric by LEE ADAMS
Music by CHARLES STROUSE

peo - ple to see; ev - 'ry - thing

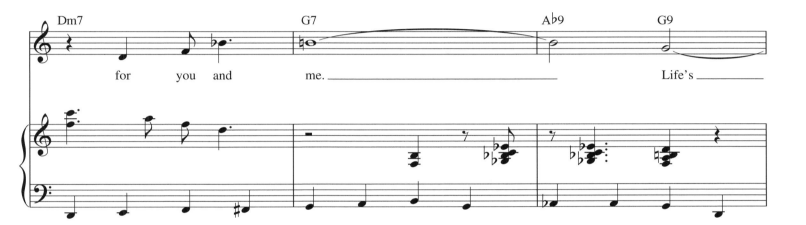

for you and me. _____ Life's _____

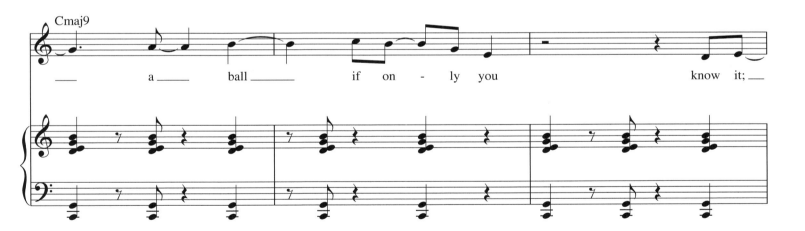

___ a ___ ball _____ if on - ly you know it; ___

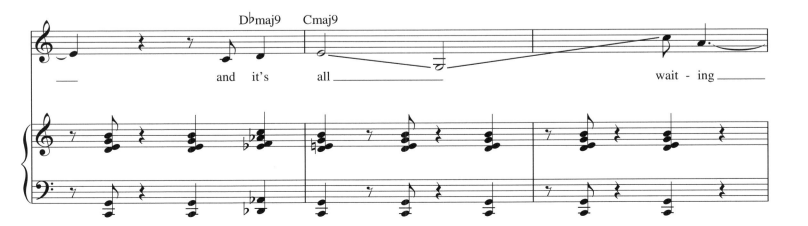

and it's all _____ wait - ing _____

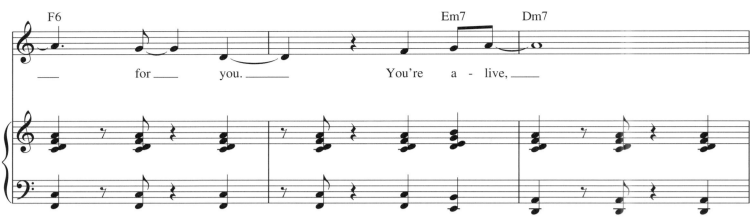

for ___ you. ___ You're a - live, ___

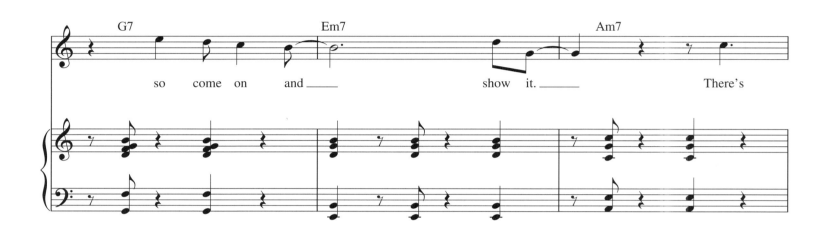

so come on and ___ show it. ___ There's

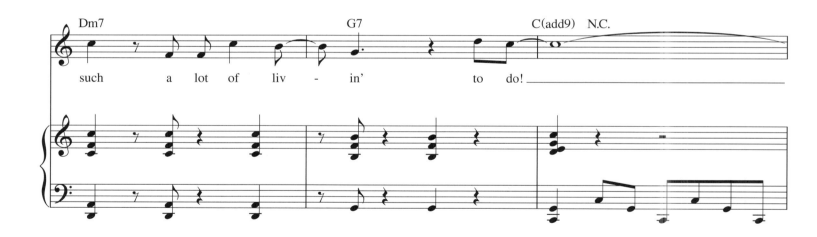

such a lot of liv - in' to do! ___

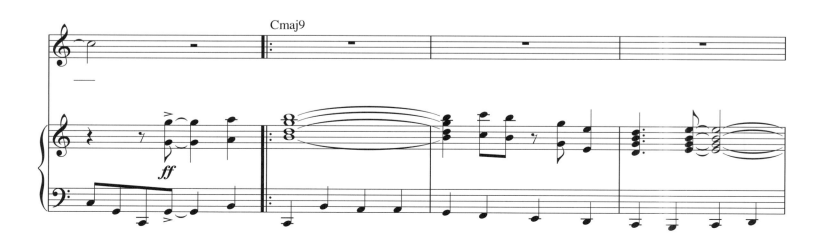

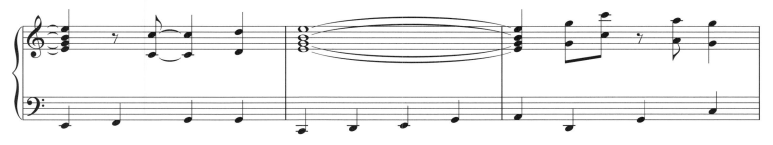

F6   Dm7   G7

Instrumental solo ad lib.
mf

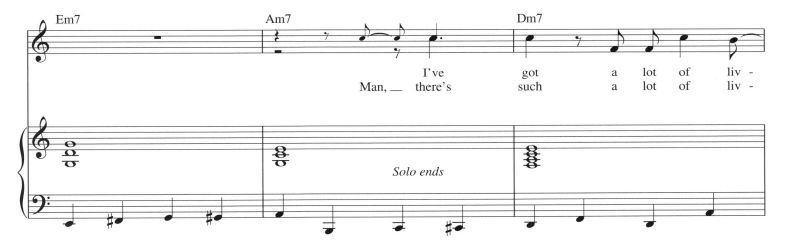

Em7   Am7   Dm7

I've   got   a   lot   of   liv -
Man, __ there's   such   a   lot   of   liv -

Solo ends

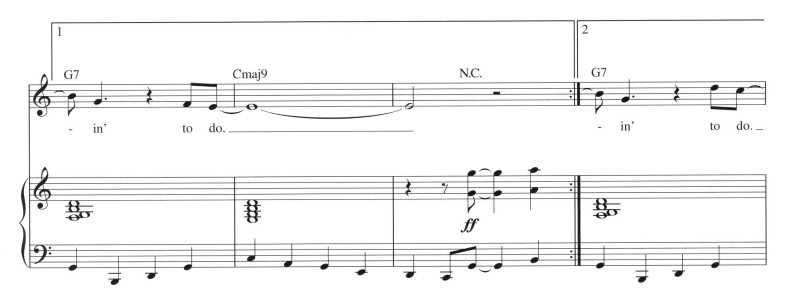

1
G7   Cmaj9   N.C.   2
                                                         G7

- in'   to do. _____   - in'   to do. _

ff

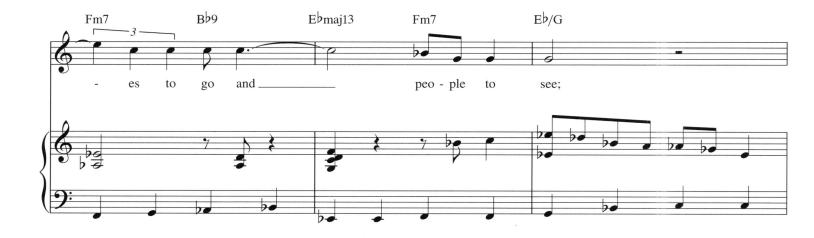

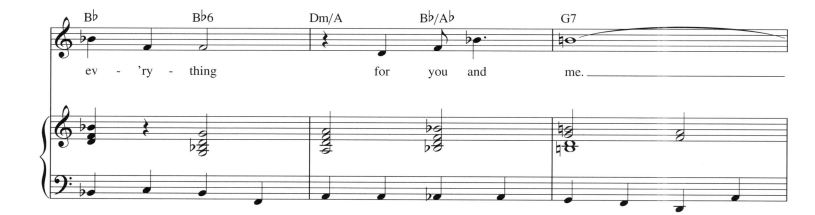

ly you'd _ know ____ it, and it's all

just wait - ing _____ for ___ you. _____ You're a - live, _

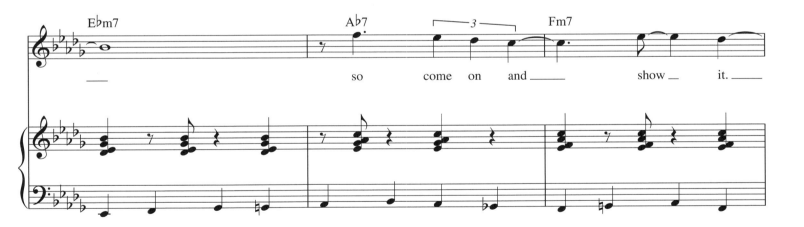

____ so come on and ____ show _ it. ____

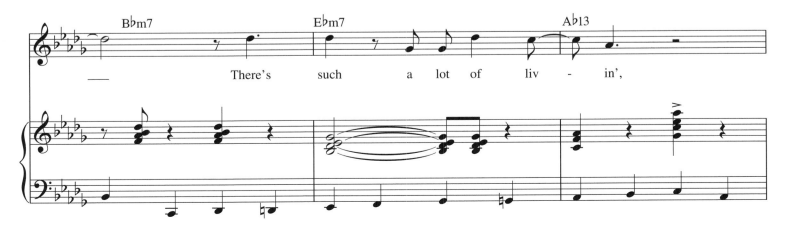

____ There's such a lot of liv - in',

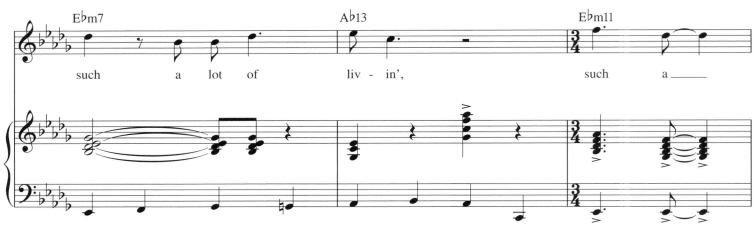

such a lot of liv-in', such a ____

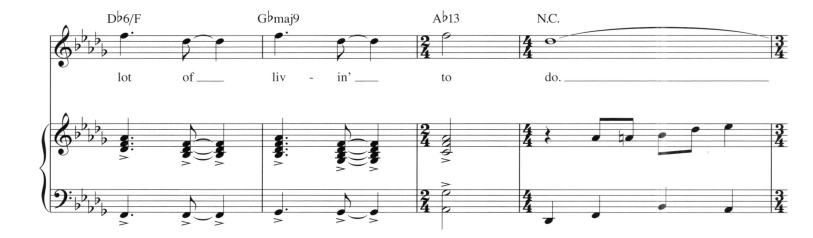

lot of ____ liv - in' ____ to do. ____

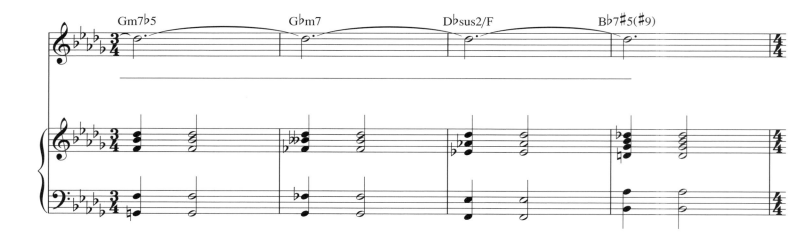

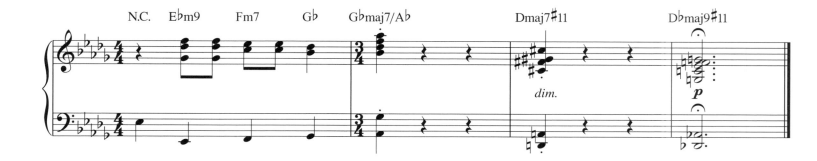

RING-A-DING DING

Words by SAMMY CAHN
Music by JAMES VAN HEUSEN

Life is ___ dull; ___ it's noth-ing but
fun-ny ___ face ___ that seemed ___ to be

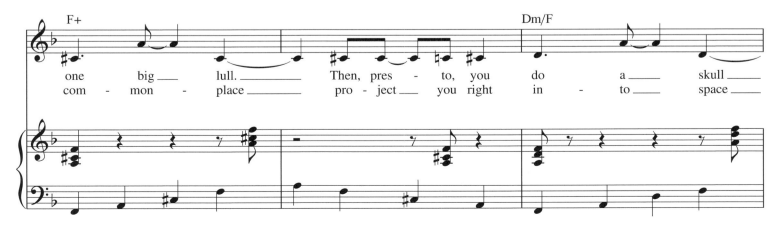

one big ___ lull. ___ Then, pres-to, you do a ___ skull ___
com-mon-place ___ pro-ject ___ you right in-to ___ space ___

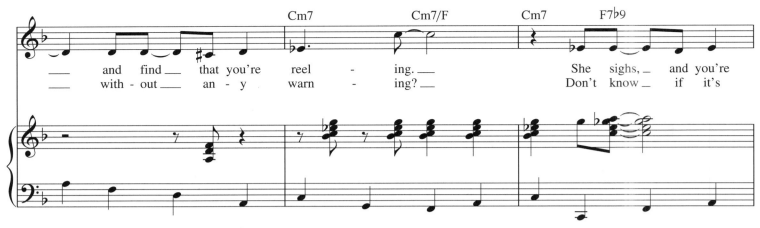

and find ___ that you're reel - ing. ___ She sighs, ___ and you're
with - out ___ an - y warn - ing? ___ Don't know ___ if it's

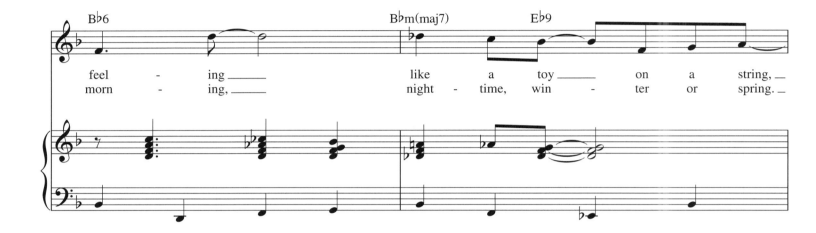

feel - ing ___ like a toy ___ on a string,
morn - ing, ___ night - time, win - ter or spring. ___

and your heart ___ goes, ring - a - ding ding, ring - a -
What's the dif - ference? Ring - a - ding ding, ring - a -

ding ding, ring - a - ding ding. How could that

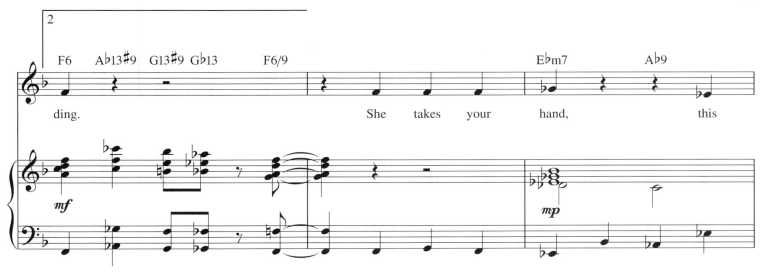

ding. She takes your hand, this

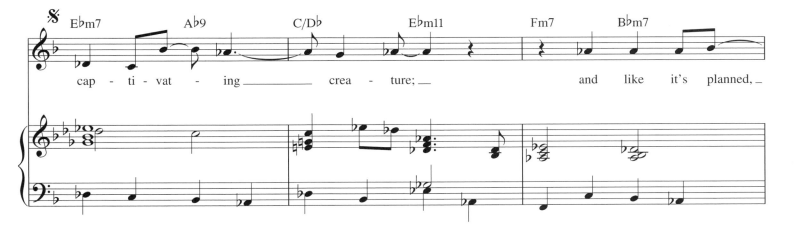

cap - ti - vat - ing _____ crea - ture; _____ and like it's planned, _

_ you're in _____ the phone _ book, look - ing _____ for the

near - est preach - er. Life is swell; _____ you're off _____ to that

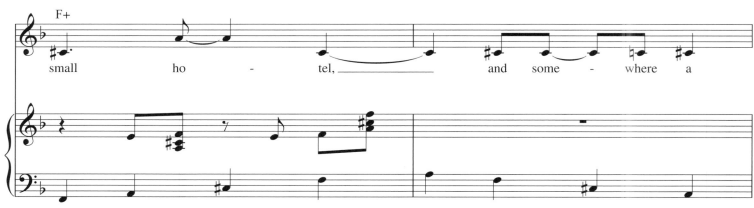

small ho - tel, _____ and some - where a

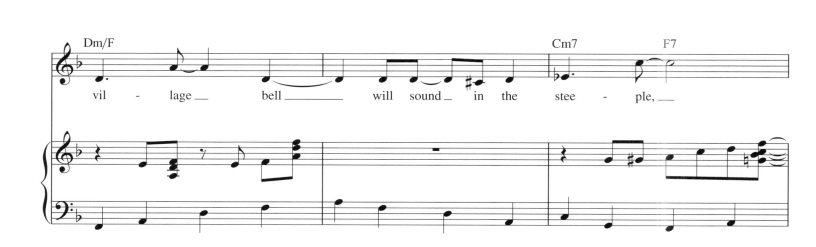

vil - lage __ bell _____ will sound _ in the stee - ple, _

an - nounc - ing to peo - ple, _ "Love's the love - li - est

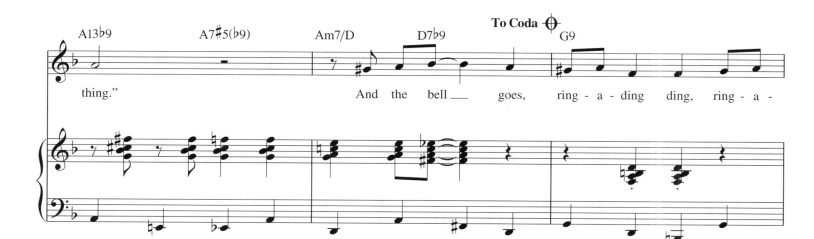

thing." And the bell __ goes, ring - a - ding ding, ring - a -

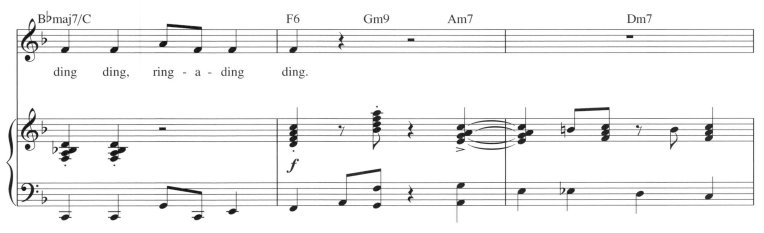

ding ding, ring - a - ding ding.

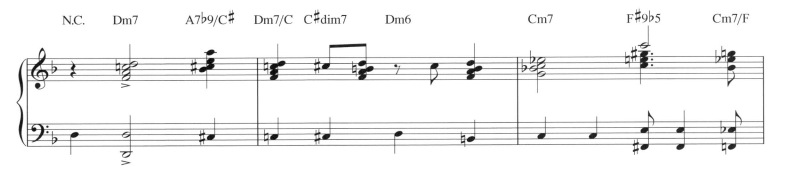

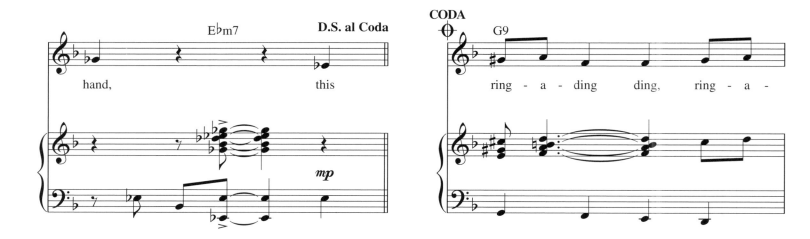

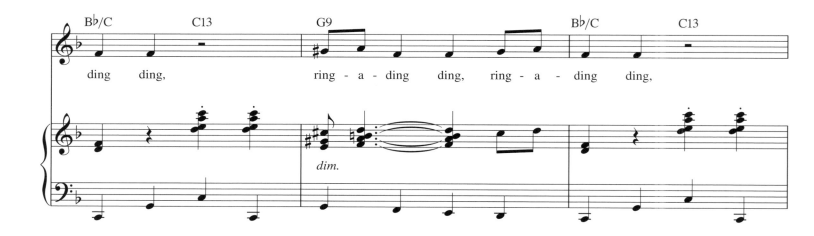

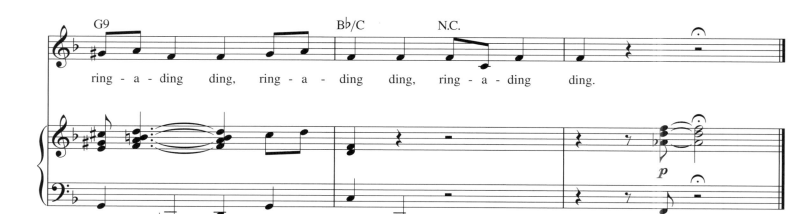

EEE-O ELEVEN

Words by SAMMY CAHN
Music by JAMES VAN HEUSEN

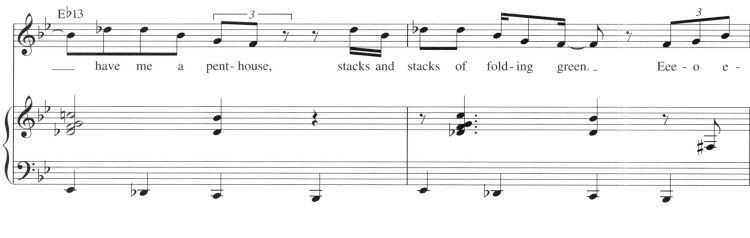

have me a pent-house, stacks and stacks of fold-ing green. ___ Eee-o e-

lev - en. Eee-o e - lev - en. It's all a

state of mind, ___ wheth-er or not you find that

place down there, or heav - en. ___ In the mean - time, Eee - o, eee-

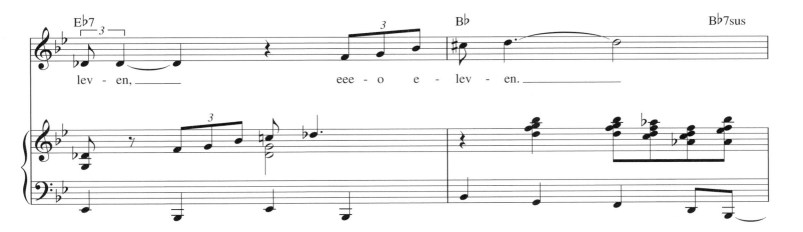

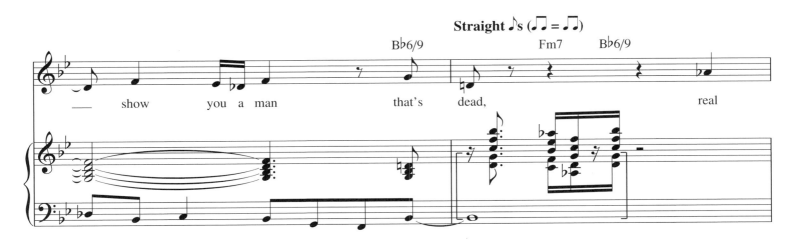

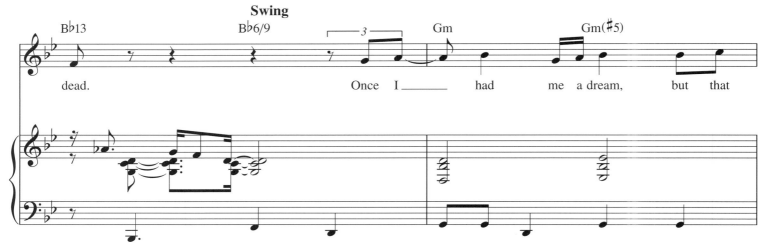

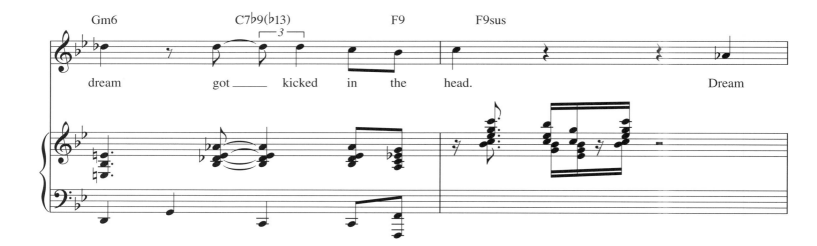

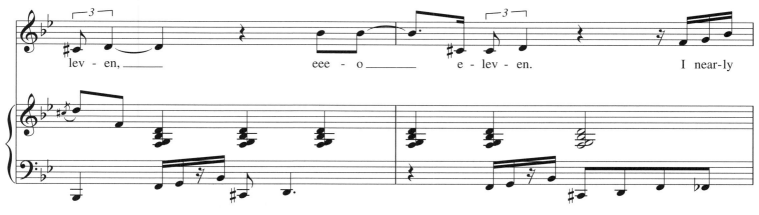

lev - en, _____ eee - o _____ e - lev - en. I near-ly

had me that pent-house, all them stacks of fold - ing green. E -

- lev - en, _____ e - lev - en. _____ Some judge is

gon - na say, _____ "I'm put - ting you a - way _____ for

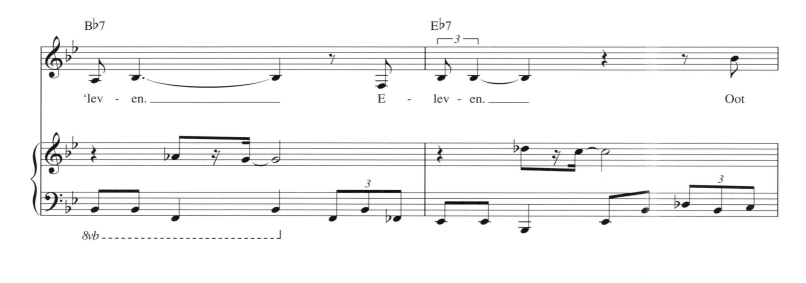

LUCK BE A LADY

from GUYS AND DOLLS

By FRANK LOESSER

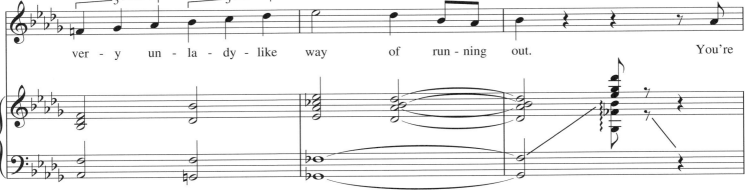

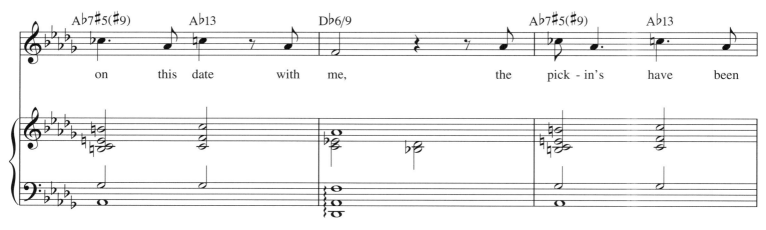

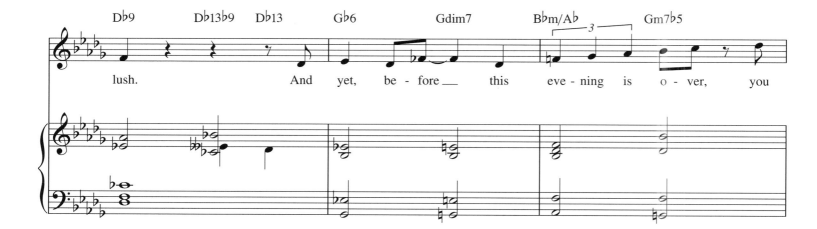

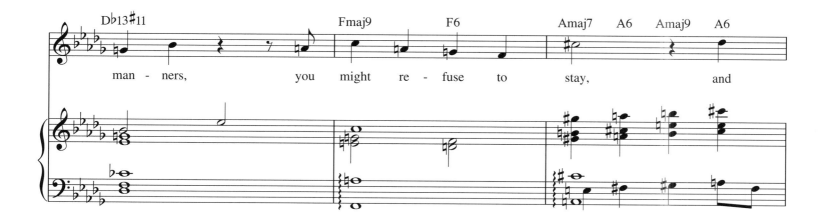

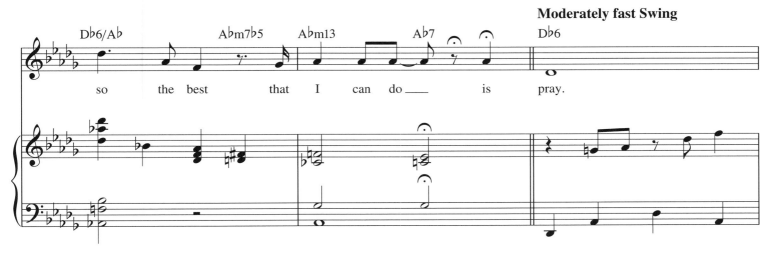

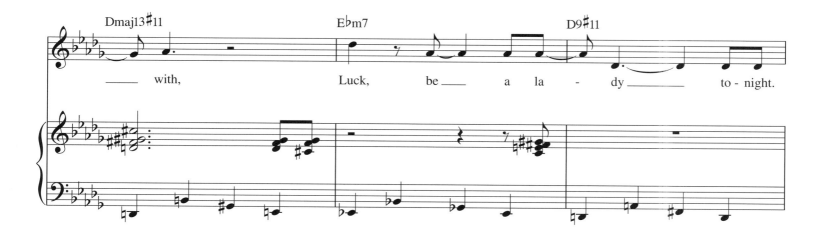

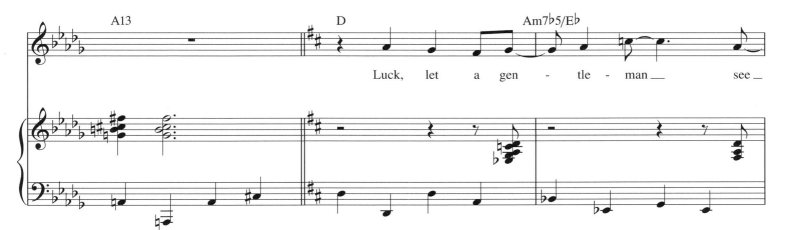

Luck, let a gen - tle - man _ see _

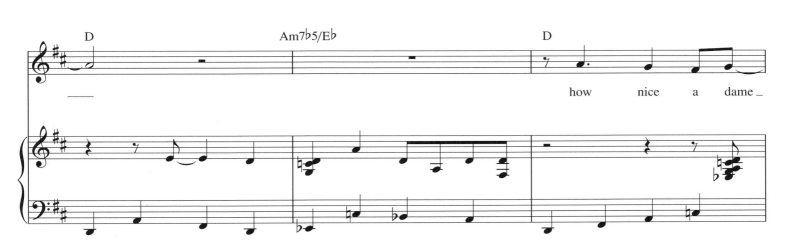

_ how nice a dame _

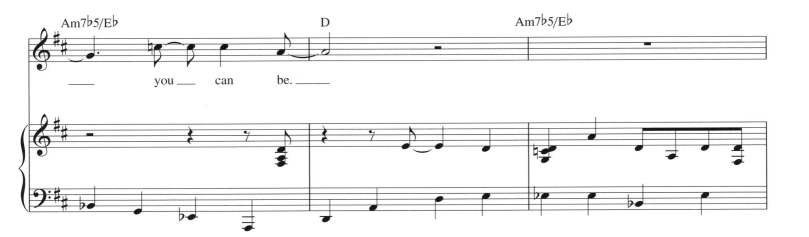

_ you _ can be. _

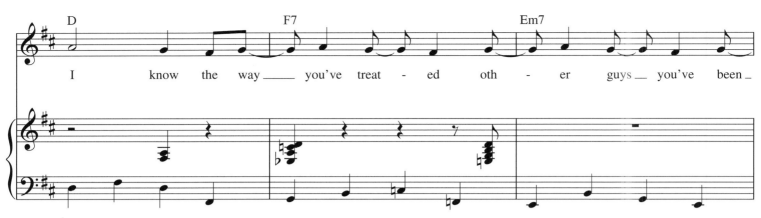

I know the way ___ you've treat - ed oth - er guys ___ you've been ___

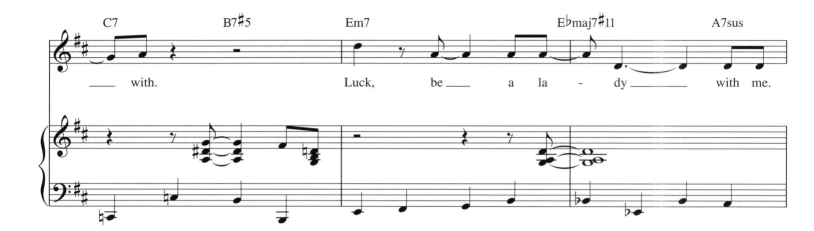

___ with. Luck, be ___ a la - dy _____ with me.

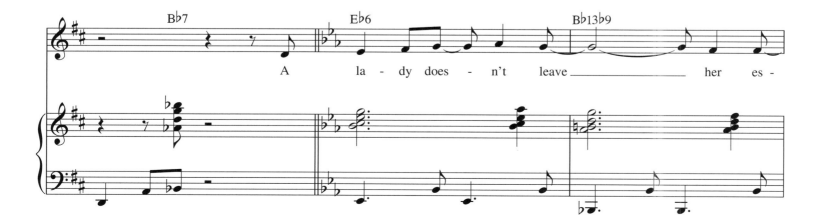

A la - dy does - n't leave _____ her es -

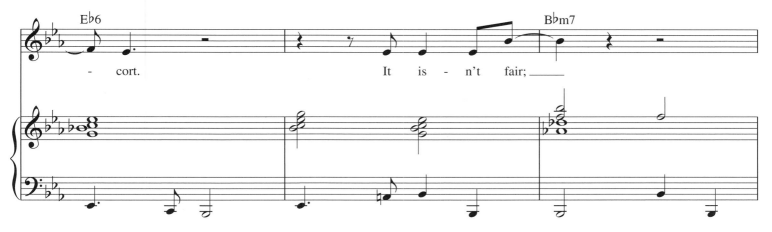

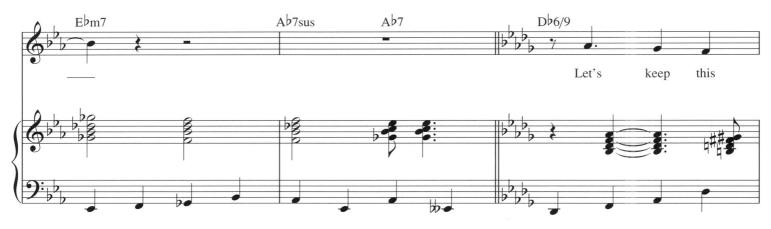

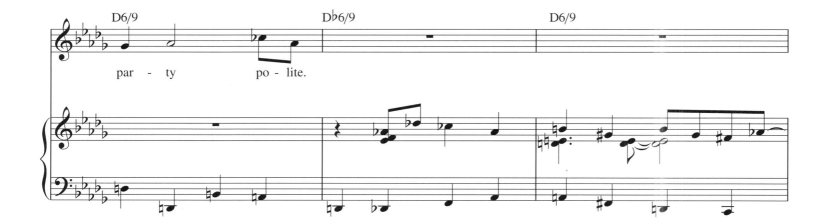

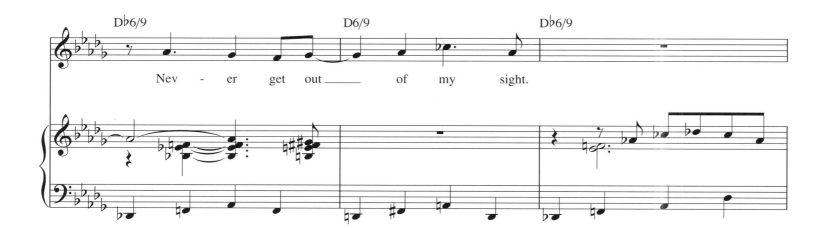

To Coda ⊕

- la you came in with. Luck, be a la-

- dy to - night.

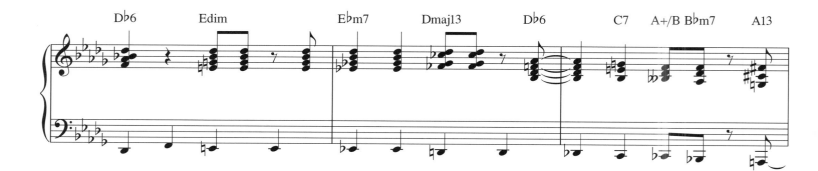

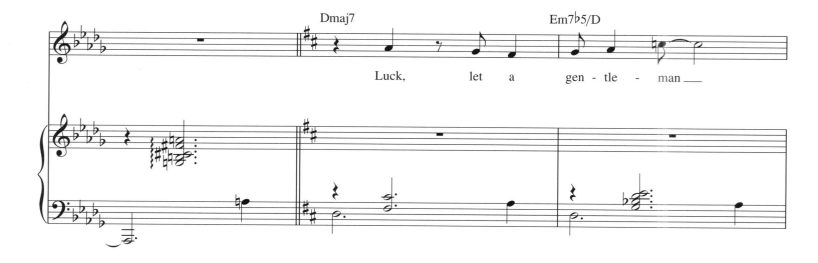

Luck, let a gen - tle - man ___

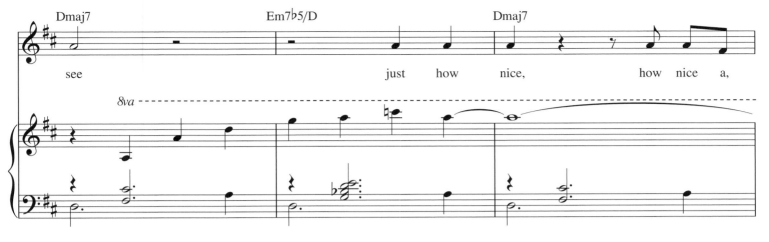

see   just how nice,   how nice a,

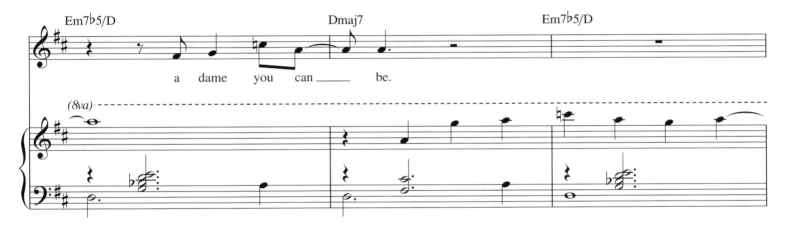

a dame you can _____ be.

I   know   the   way _____ you've treat - ed oth - er guys _ you've been _

D.S. al Coda

_____ with.   Hey,   luck,   be   a   la - dy _____ with me.

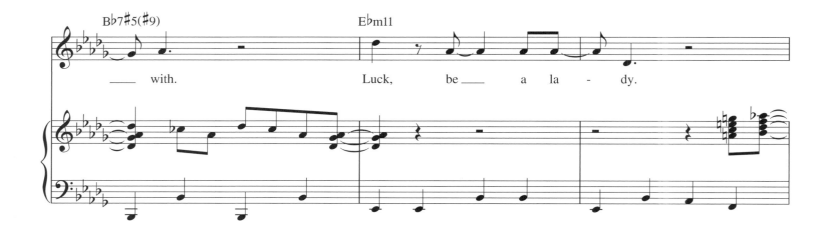

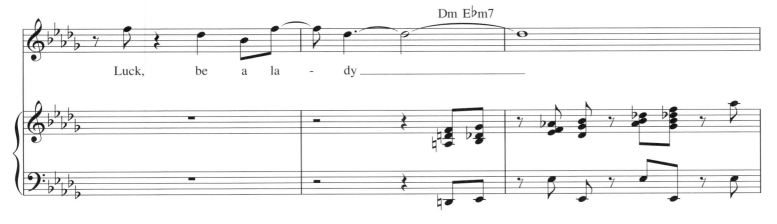

Luck, be a la - dy _____

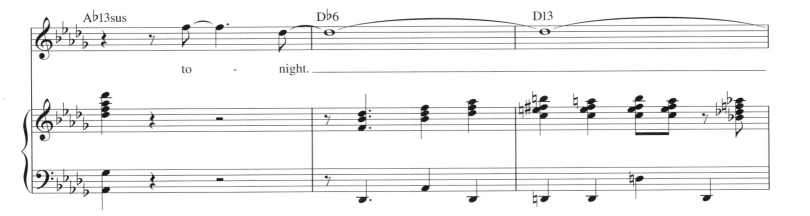

to - night. _____

VOLARE

Music by DOMENICO MODUGNO
Original Italian Text by D. MODUGNO
and F. MIGLIACCI
English lyric by MITCHELL PARISH

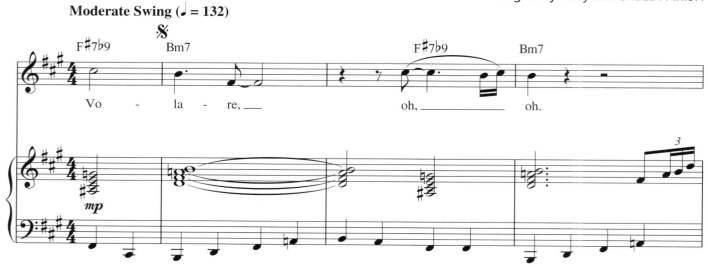

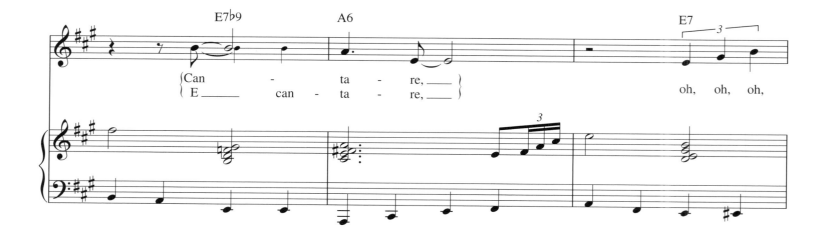

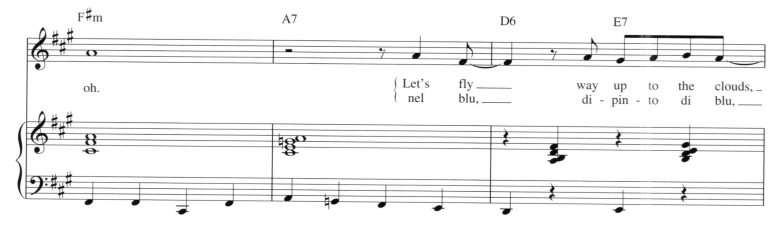

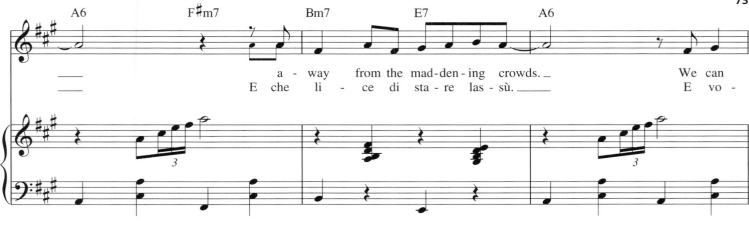

a - way from the mad-den-ing crowds. ___ We can
E che li - ce di sta - re las - sù. ___ E vo -

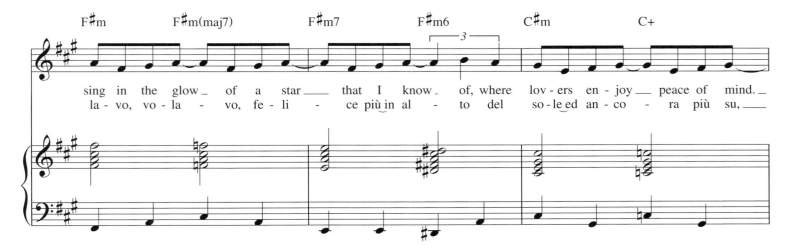

sing in the glow ___ of a star ___ that I know ___ of, where lov-ers en - joy ___ peace of mind. ___
la-vo, vo - la - vo, fe - li - ce più in al - to del so - le ed an - co - ra più su, ___

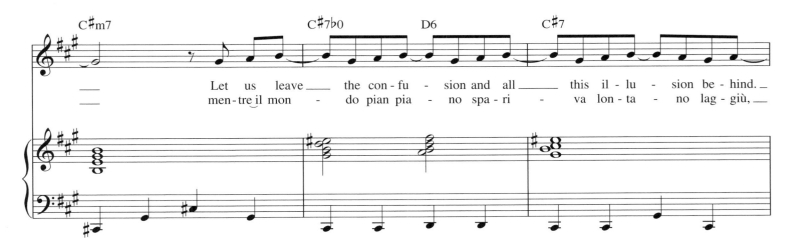

Let us leave ___ the con - fu - sion and all ___ this il - lu - sion be - hind. ___
men-tre il mon - do pian pia - no spa - ri - va lon - ta - no lag - giù, ___

Just like birds of a fea - ther, a
u - na mu - si - ca dol - ce suo -

rain - bow to - geth - er we'll find.___
na - va sol - tan - to per me.___

Vo -

la - re, ___ oh, ___ oh.

E ___ can - ta - re, ___ oh, oh, oh,

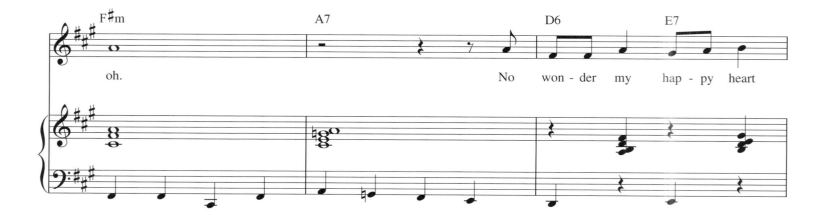

oh.

No won - der my hap - py heart

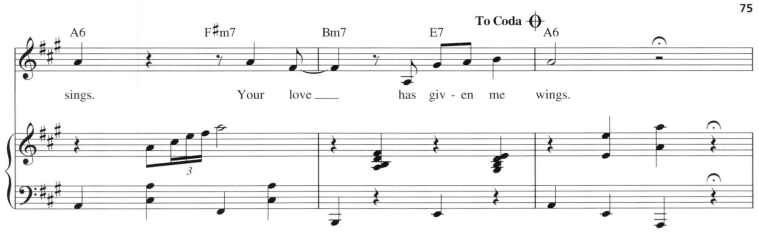

sings. Your love ___ has giv-en me wings.

Slowly, very freely

Pen - so che un sog - no co - sì non ri - tor - ni mai più: ___

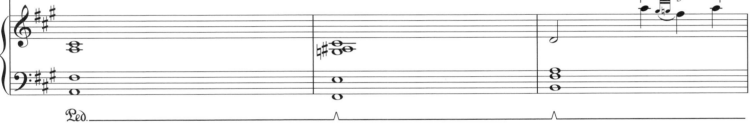

mi di - pin - ge - vo le ma - ni e la fac - cia di

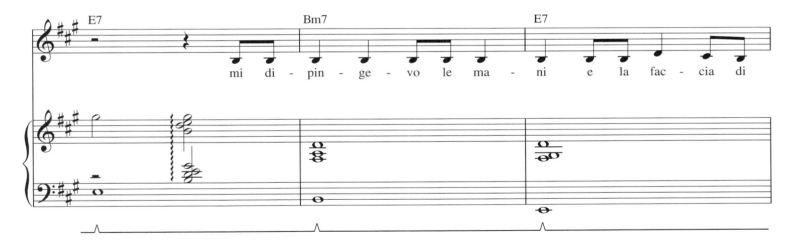

blu, ___ poi d'im - prov - vi - so ve -

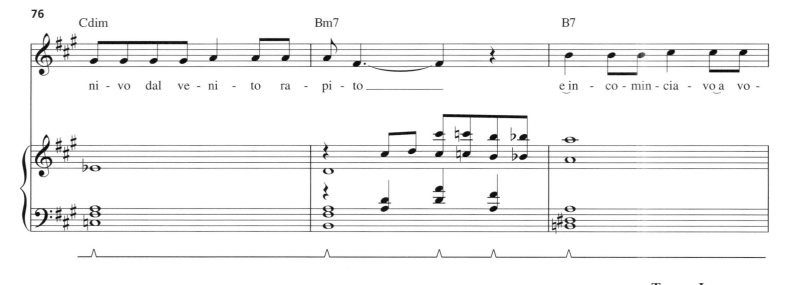

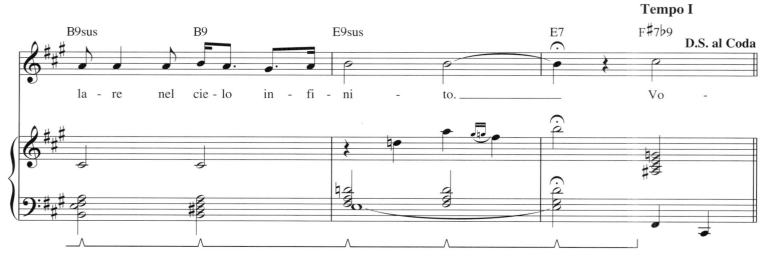

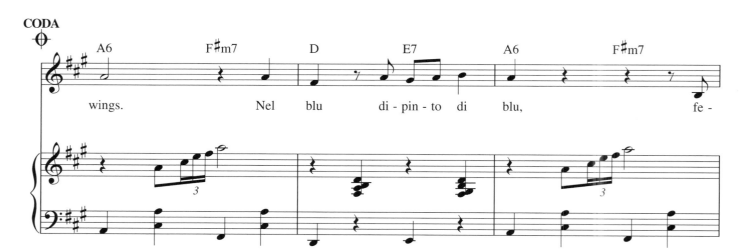

THE BIRTH OF THE BLUES

Words by B.G. DeSYLVA
and LEW BROWN
Music by RAY HENDERSON

Moderate Blues tempo

With pedal

Freely

Oh, _____ they say some peo-ple long a-go
so, _____ they start-ed sway-in' to and fro.

were look-ing for _____ a dif-f'rent tune, one that they could
They did-n't know _____ just what to use, but this is how the

croon as on-ly they can. _____ They on-ly had _ the rhy-thm,
blues real-ly be -

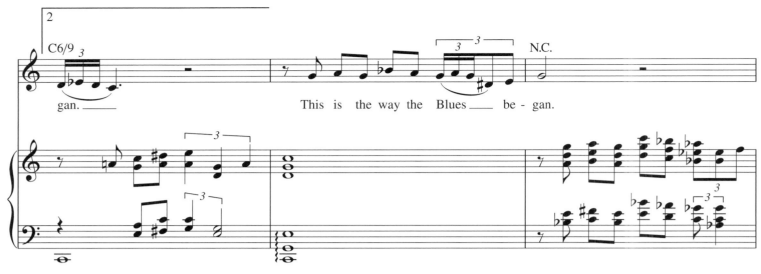

This is the way the Blues ___ be-gan.

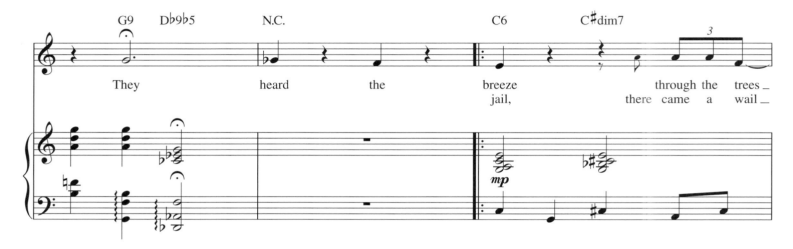

They heard the breeze jail, through the trees ___ there came a wail ___

sing-ing weird mel-o-dies, ___ and ___ they
from a down-heart-ed frail, ___ and ___ they

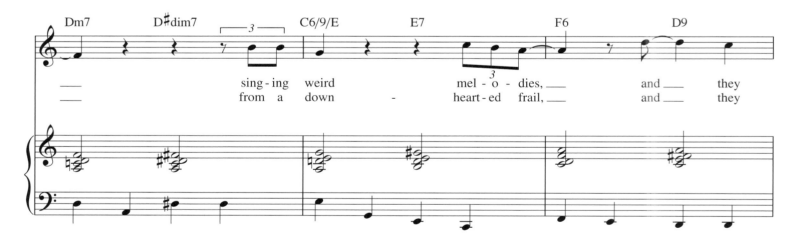

named that just the start of the Blues. ___
played that as a part of the Blues. ___

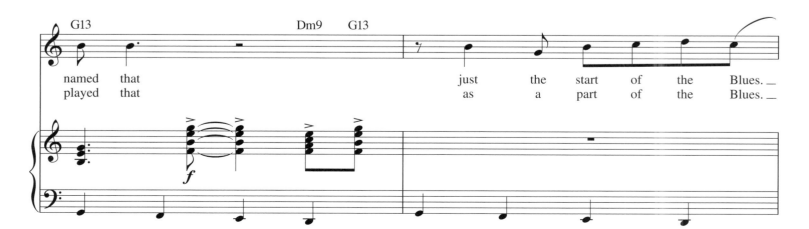

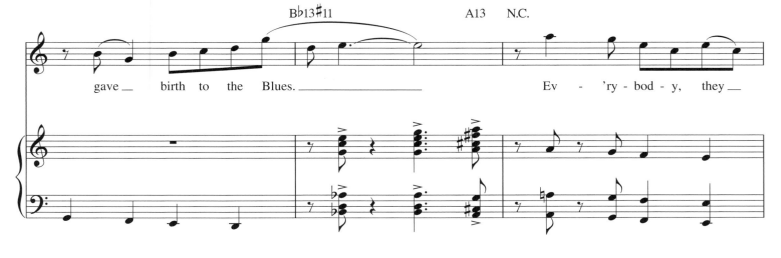

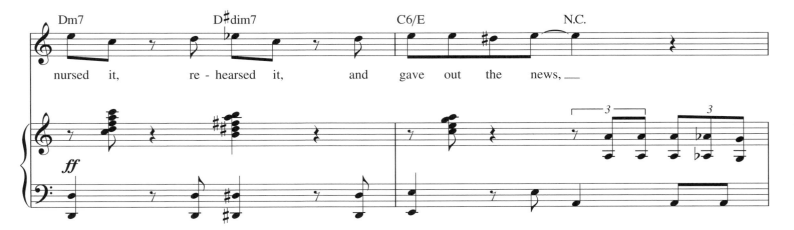

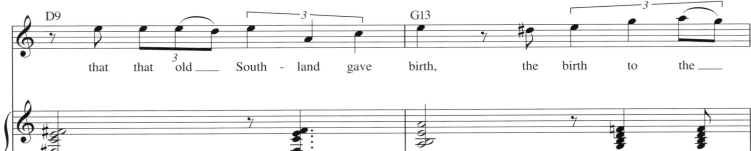

WITCHCRAFT

Music by CY COLEMAN
Lyrics by CAROLYN LEIGH

Those fin- gers in my hair, ___

that sly, _____ "come hith- er" stare ___ strips my

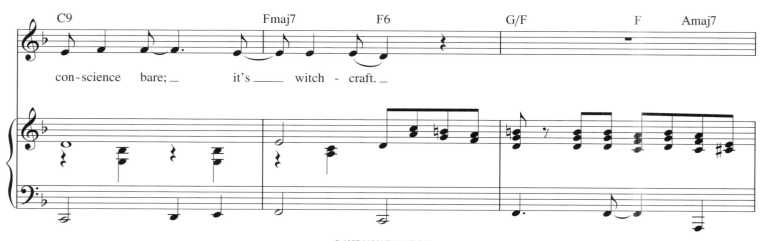

con- science bare; ___ it's ___ witch- craft. ___

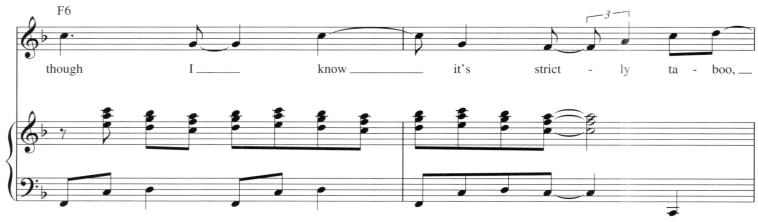

though I _____ know _____ it's strict - ly ta - boo, _____

_____ when you a - rouse _____

_____ the need in me, _____ my heart _____ says, _____ "Yes in - deed," in me.

Pro - ceed with what you're lead - ing me to. _____

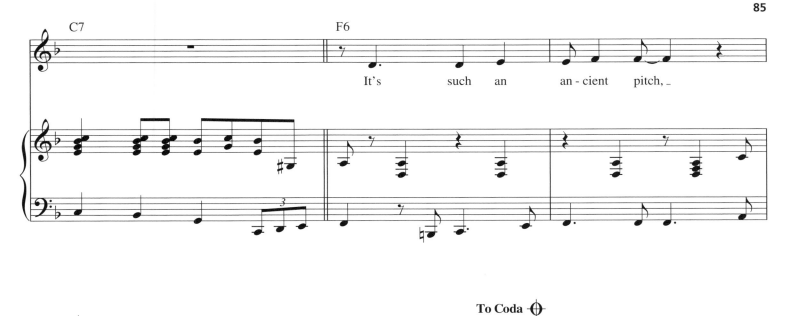

It's such an an-cient pitch, _

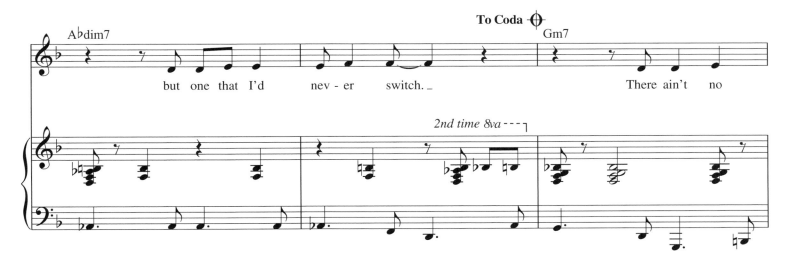

To Coda ⊕

but one that I'd nev-er switch. _ There ain't no

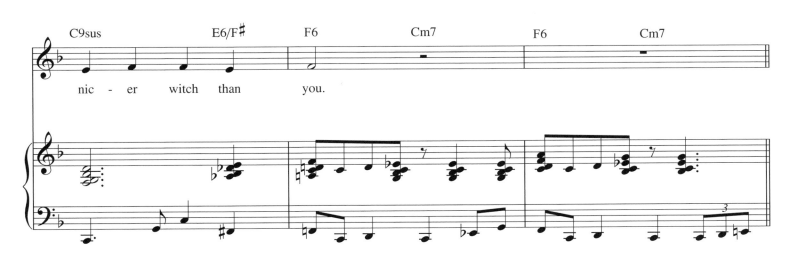

nic - er witch than you.

YOU'RE NOBODY 'TIL SOMEBODY LOVES YOU

Words and Music by RUSS MORGAN,
LARRY STOCK and JAMES CAVANAUGH

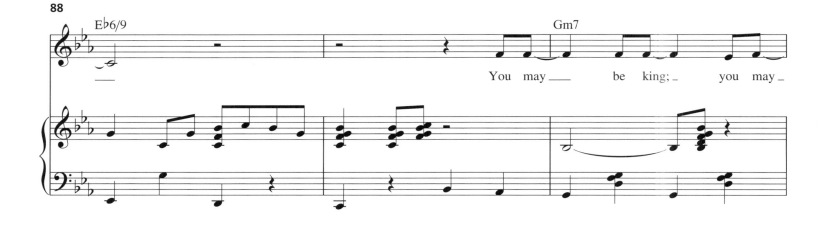

You may ___ be king; you may ___

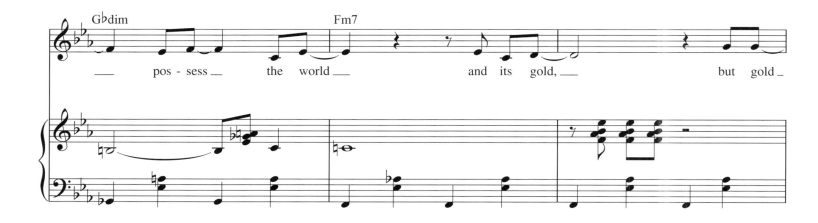

___ pos - sess ___ the world ___ and its gold, ___ but gold ___

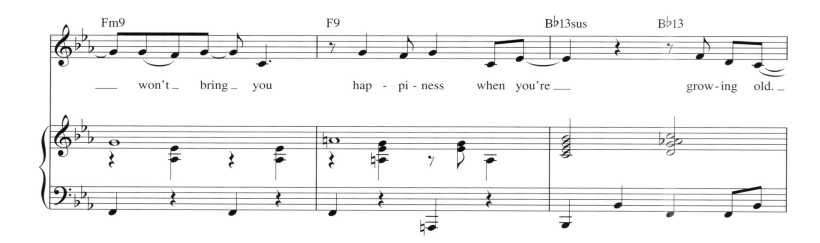

___ won't ___ bring ___ you hap - pi - ness when you're ___ grow - ing old. ___

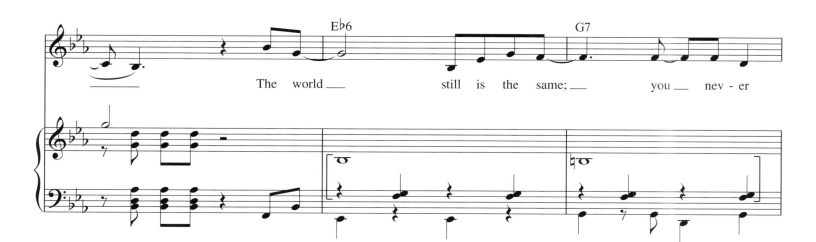

The world ___ still is the same; ___ you ___ nev - er

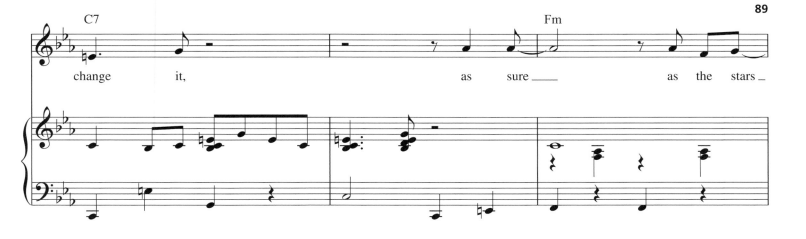

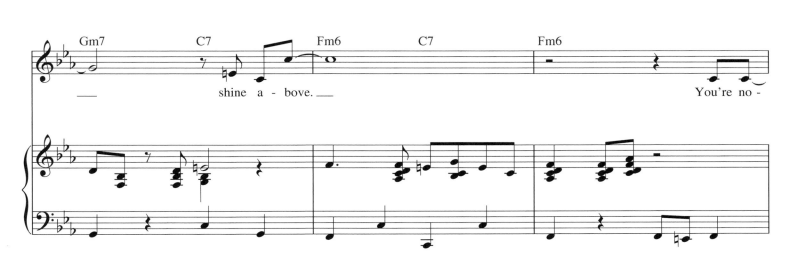

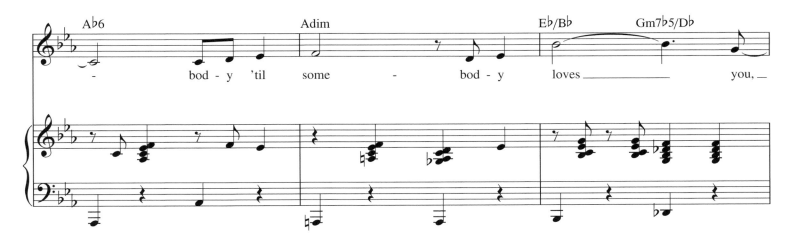

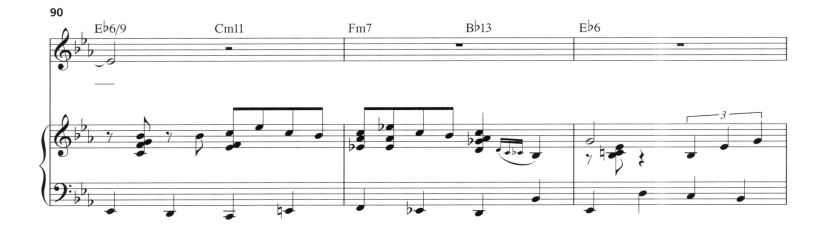

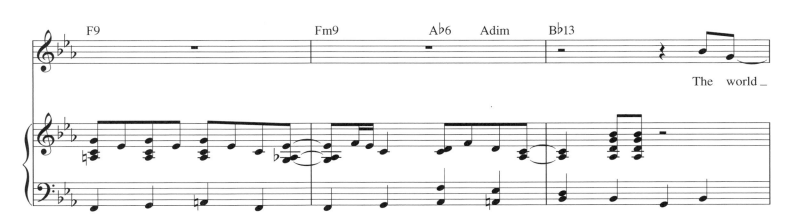

The world —

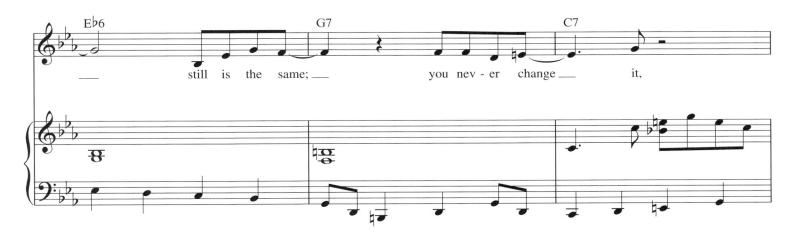

still is the same; — you nev - er change — it,

as sure ____ as the stars _____ shine a -

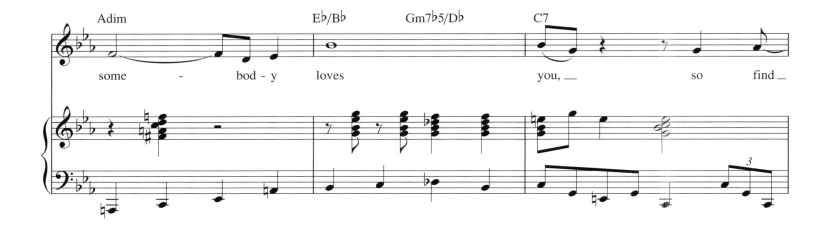

I GET A KICK OUT OF YOU

Words and Music by
COLE PORTER

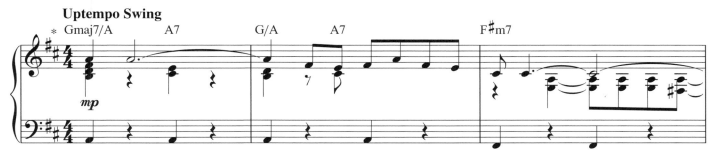

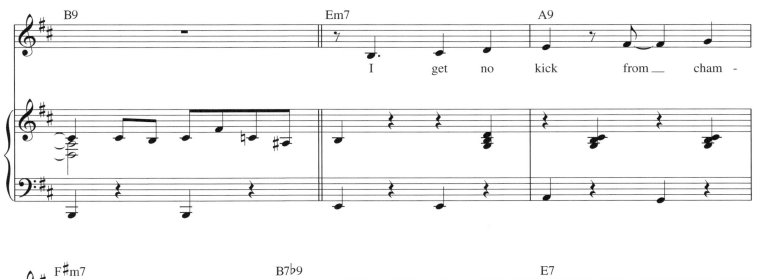

* *Recorded a half step lower.*

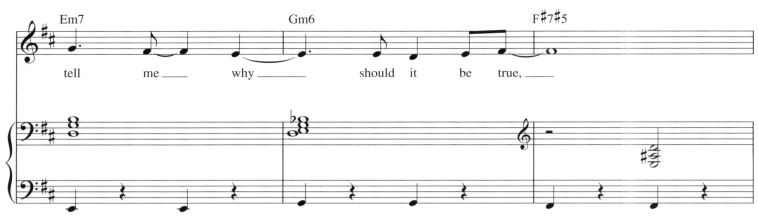

tell me ____ why _____ should it be true, ____

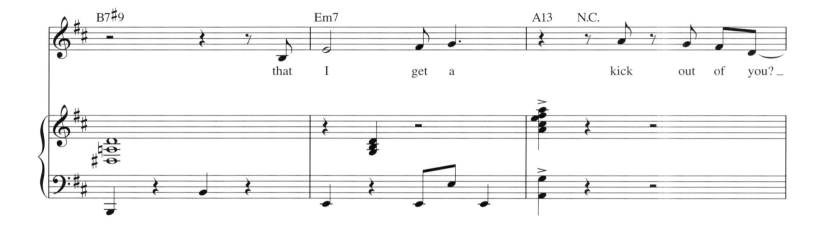

that I get a kick out of you? _

Some __ like the

bop - type re - frain; ___

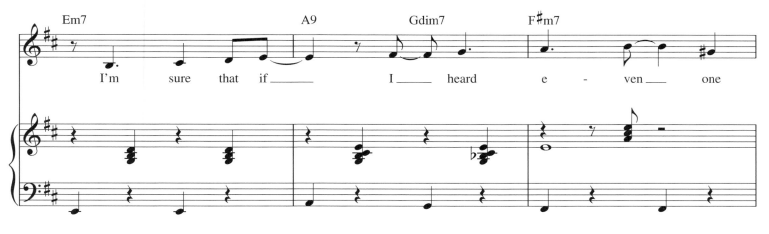

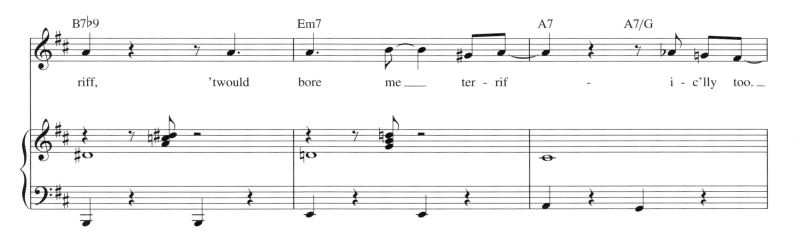

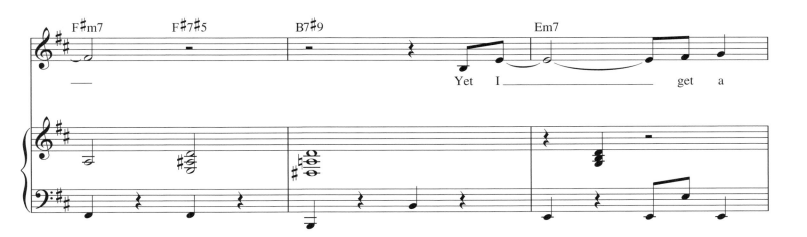

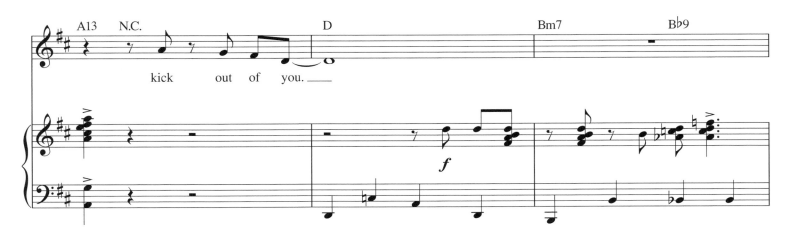

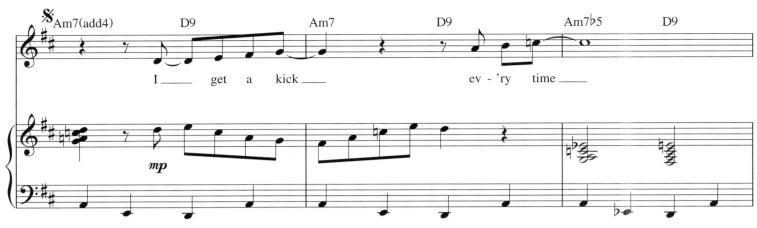

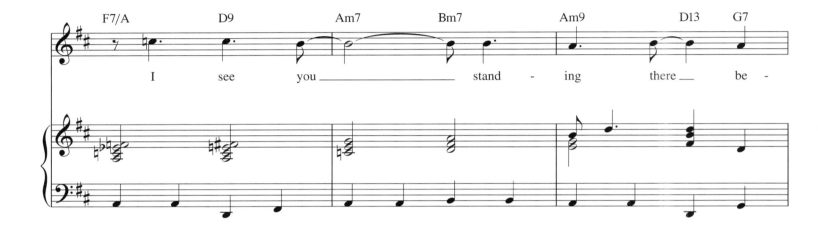

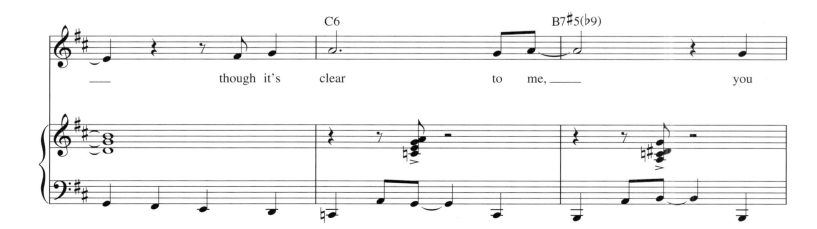

ob - vi - ous - ly　　　　　do　not　a - dore _____ me.

To Coda ⊕

____　　　I　get　no　kick　　in　a　plane; _

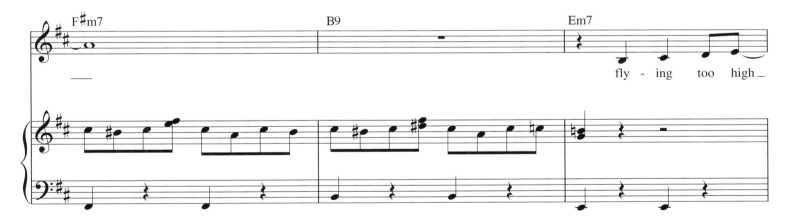

fly - ing　too　high _

____　　with　some ___ gal ____　in　the　sky ____　　　is ___

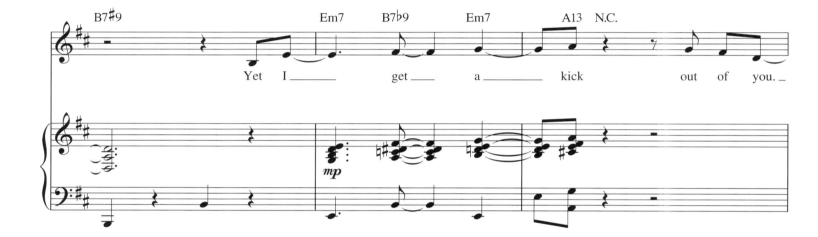

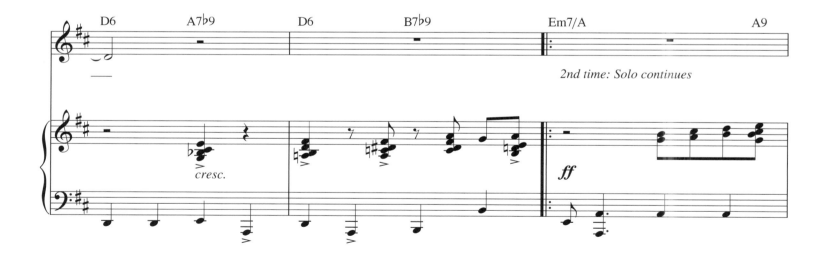

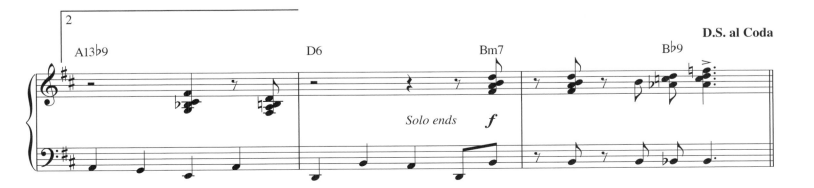

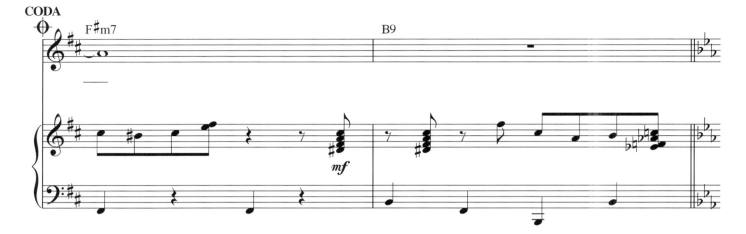

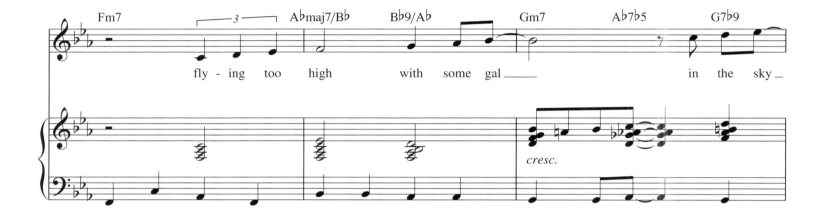

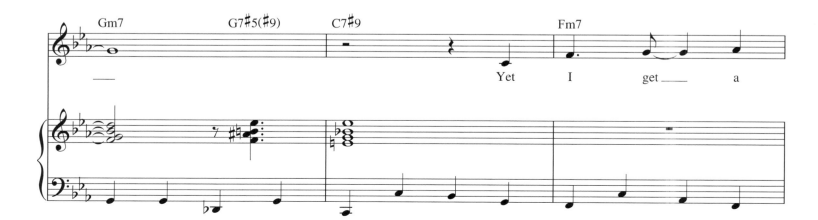

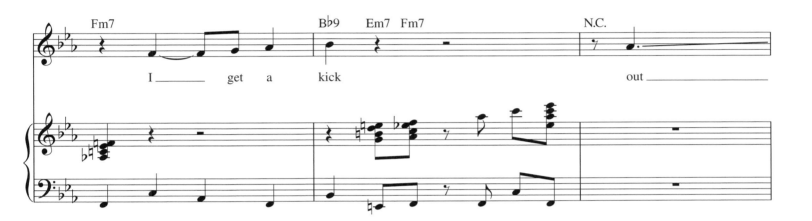

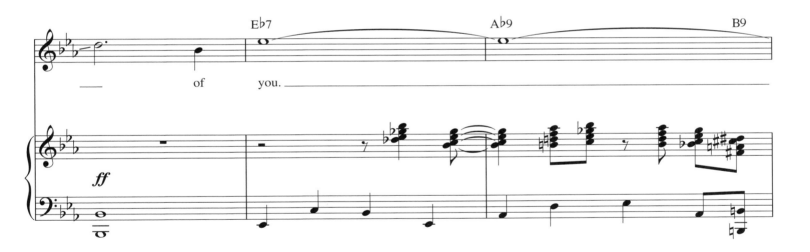

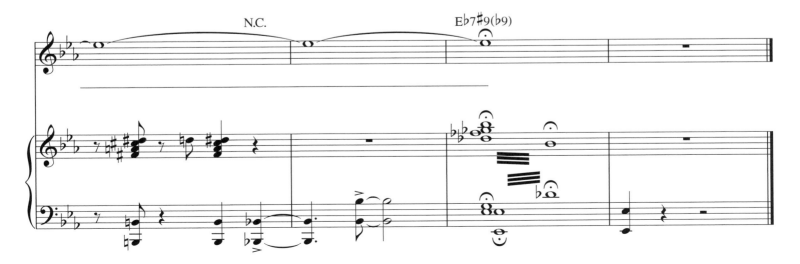

SAM'S SONG

Words by JACK ELLIOTT
Music by LEW QUADLING

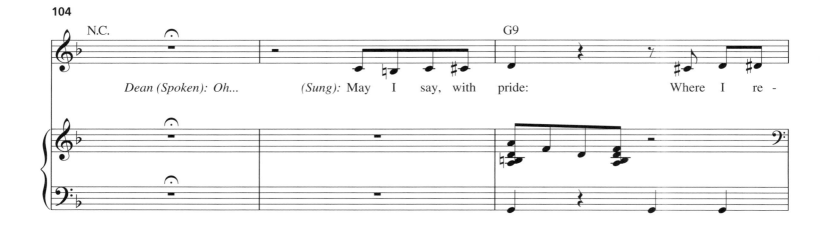

Dean (Spoken): Oh...   (Sung): May I say, with pride: Where I re-

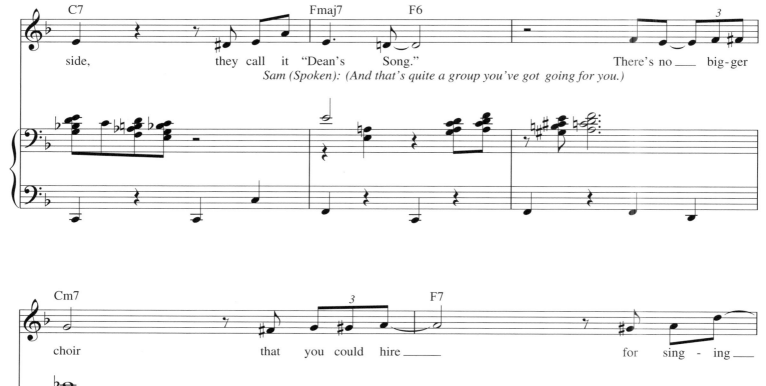

side,   they call it "Dean's   Song."   There's no ___ big-ger

Sam (Spoken): (And that's quite a group you've got going for you.)

choir   that you could hire _____   for sing - ing ___

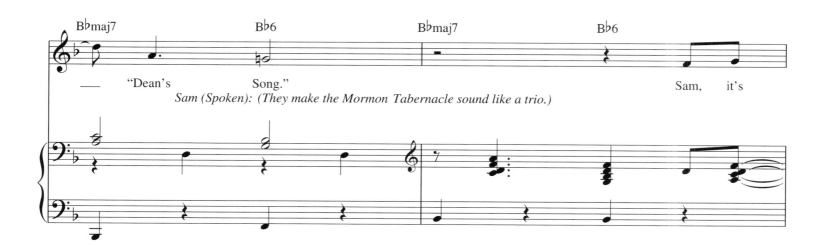

___ "Dean's   Song."   Sam, it's

Sam (Spoken): (They make the Mormon Tabernacle sound like a trio.)

say - ing you're be - ing un - kind, 'cause you're call - ing it...) *Dean:* "Clyde's Song."

Sam: My I - tal - ian friend, ___ we have

reached the end. ___ We simp - ly don't seem to

blend. *Dean:* Sam, let's ___ com - pro - mise.
Sam:(Oh, I hear what you say, but by that do you

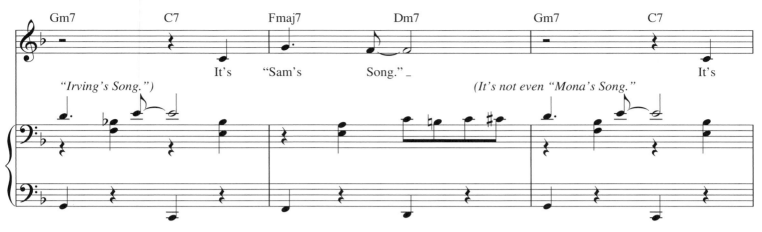

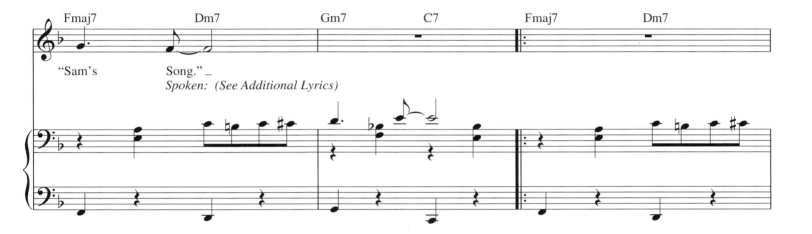

Additional Lyrics

Sam: Only thing I know is, when this record come out,
                  it better have "Sam's Song" on it, or else you gonna get a nasty letter
                  from Calhoun, and a telephone call too.

Dean: Yeah, I think you starting to get dirty now over there.

Sam: Oui! We gonna have a meeting at the lodge hall. You wanna come by a little
                  later on?

Dean: Well, you gotta ask me the right way...

I'M GONNA LIVE TILL I DIE

Words and Music by AL HOFFMAN,
WALTER KENT and MANNY KURTZ

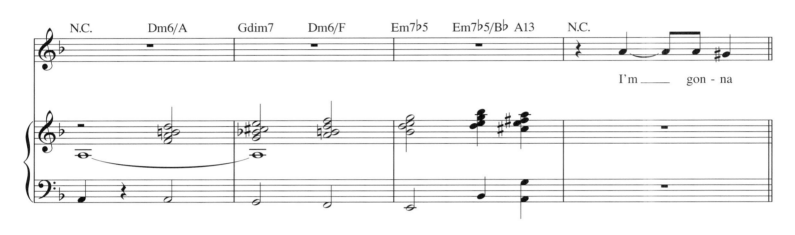

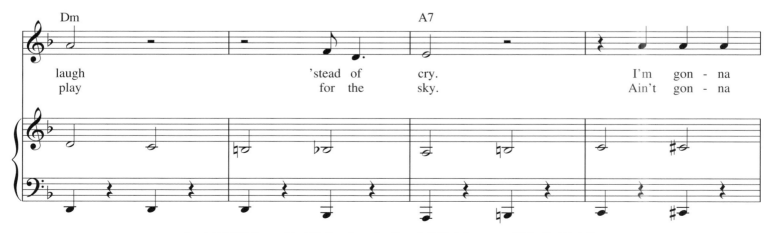

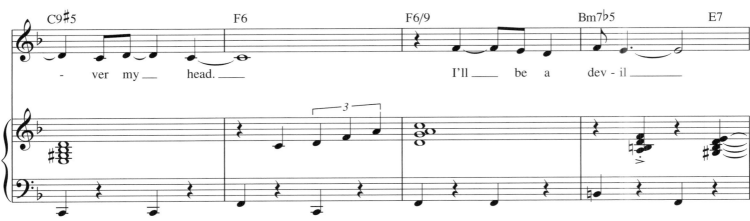

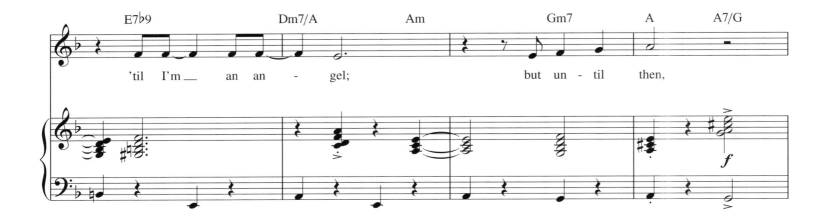

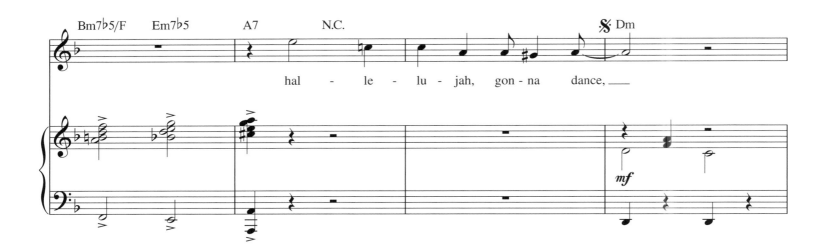

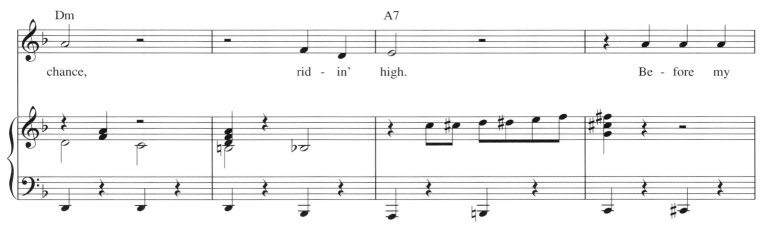

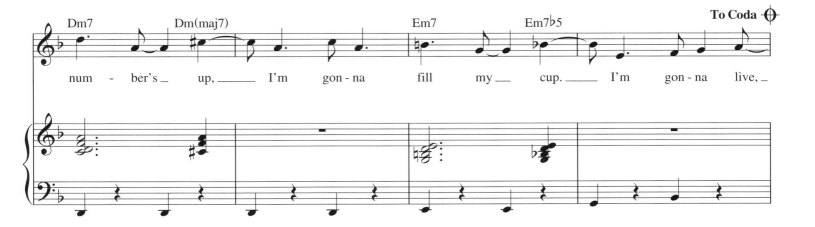

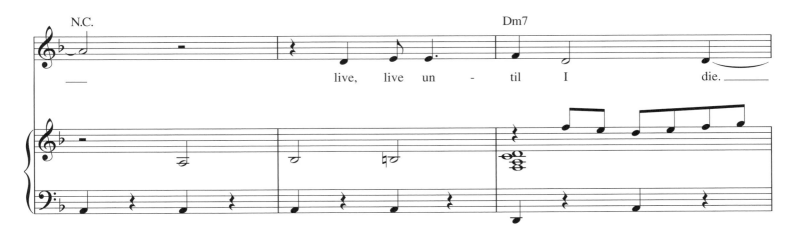

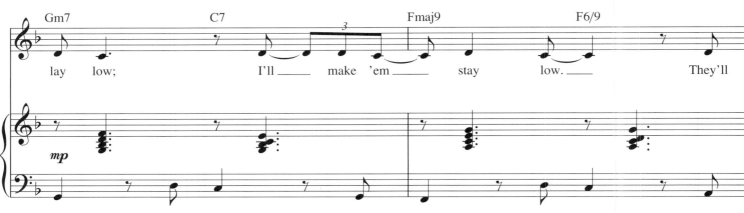

lay low; I'll ___ make 'em ___ stay low. ___ They'll

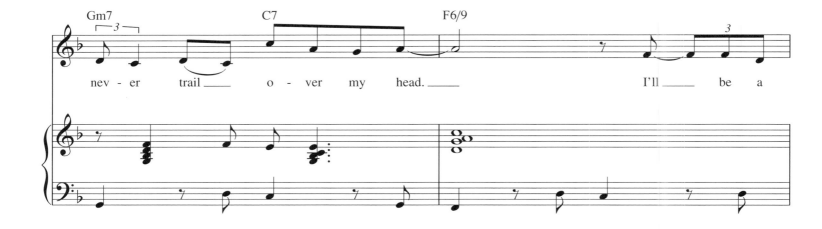

nev - er trail ___ o - ver my head. ___ I'll ___ be a

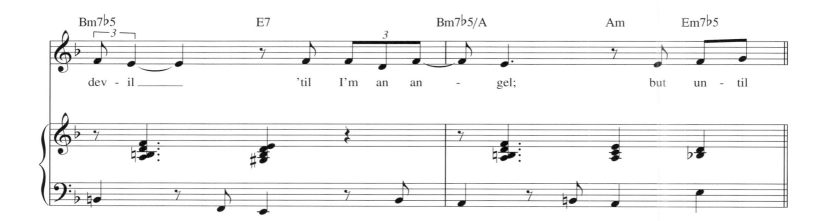

dev - il ___ 'til I'm an an - gel; but un - til

then, hal - le - lu - jah, gon - na dance; _

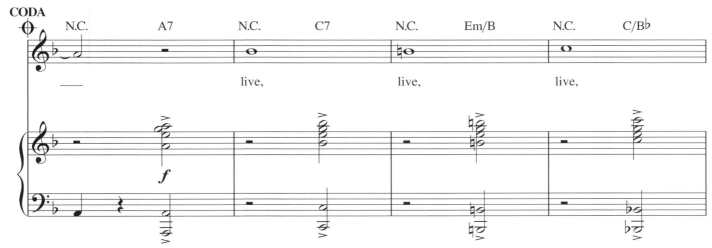

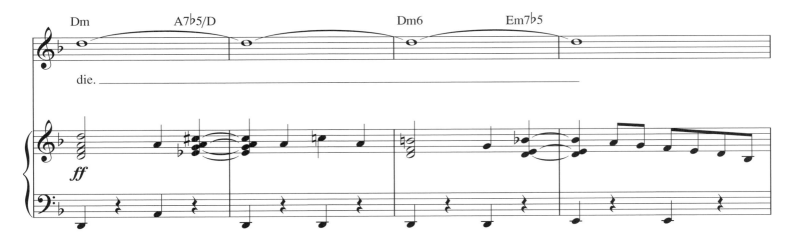

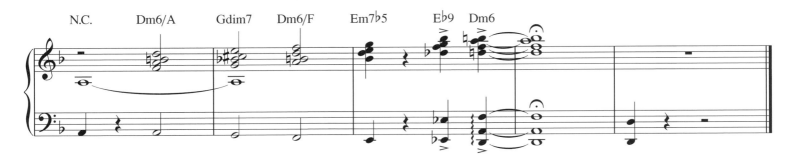

EVERYBODY LOVES SOMEBODY

Words by IRVING TAYLOR
Music by KEN LANE

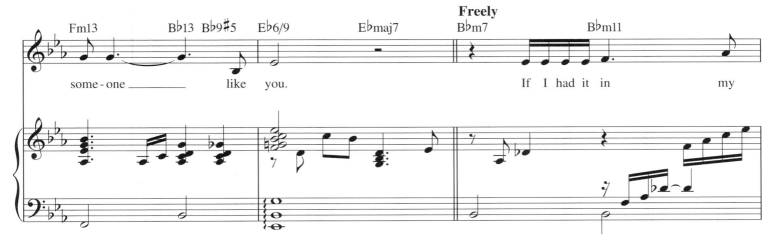

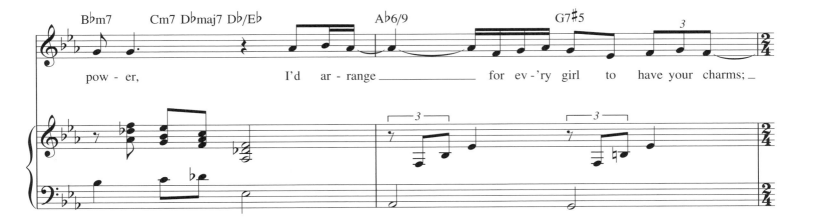

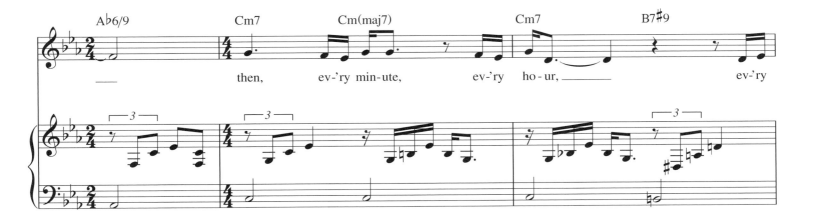

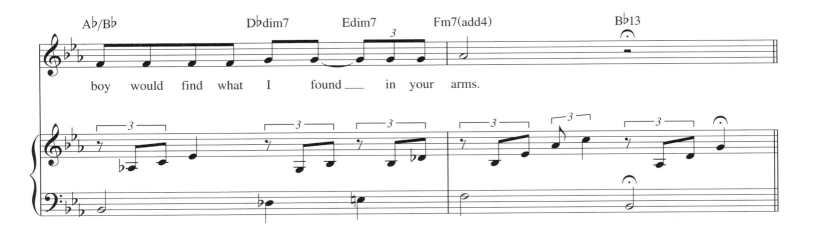

Tempo I

Ev - 'ry - bod - y loves ____ some-bod - y some - time;

and al - though my dream was o - ver - due,

your love ____ made it well worth wait - ing for

Freely

some-one like you. ____

ME AND MY SHADOW

Words by BILLY ROSE
Music by AL JOLSON
and DAVE DREYER

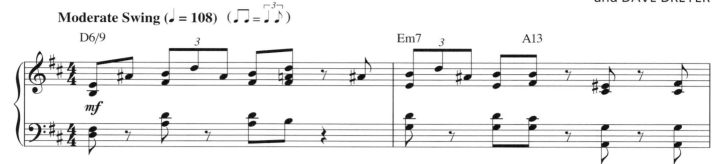

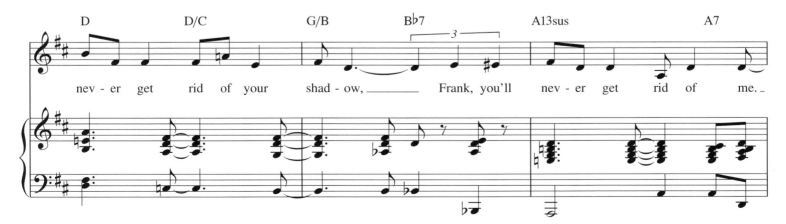

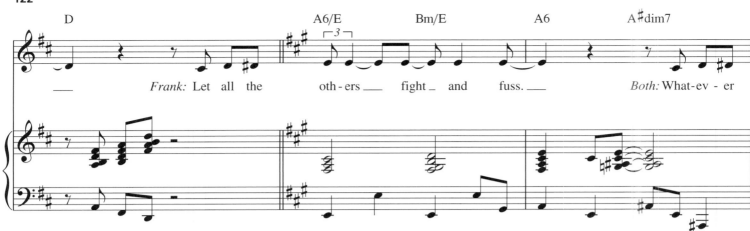

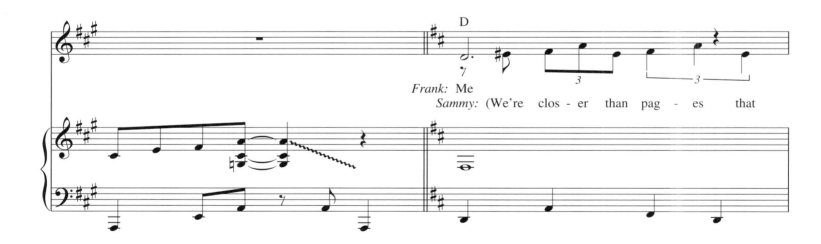

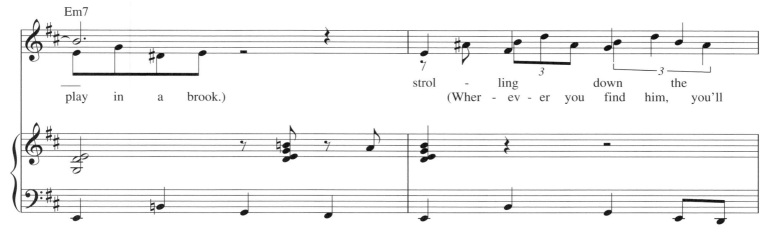

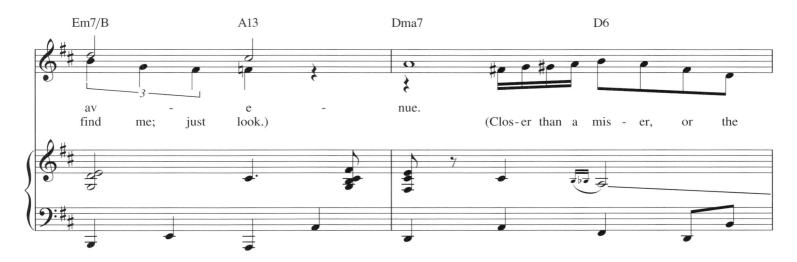

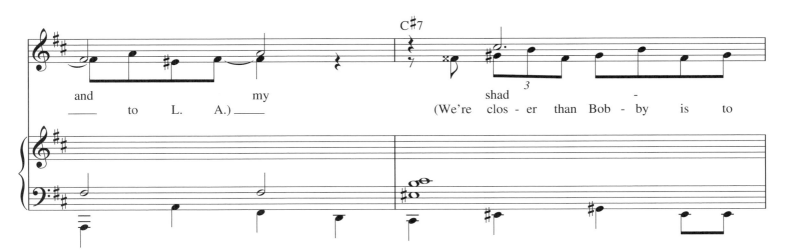

make the town roar. ___ We'll make all the late spots, and
men - tion a few, ___ we'll drop in at Dan - ny's, the

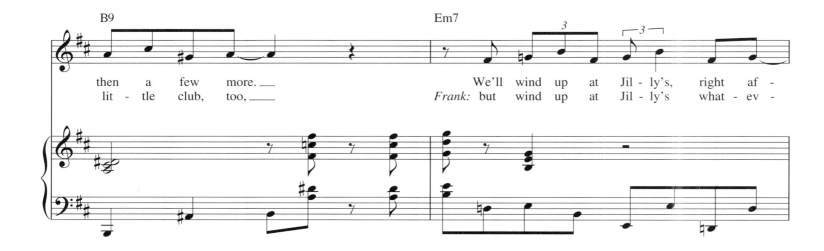

then a few more. ___ We'll wind up at Jil - ly's, right af -
lit - tle club, too, ___ *Frank:* but wind up at Jil - ly's what - ev -

To Coda ⊕

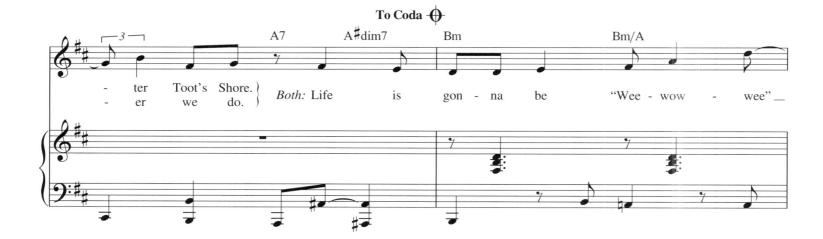

- ter Toot's Shore. *Both:* Life is gon - na be "Wee - wow - wee" ___
- er we do.

___ for my

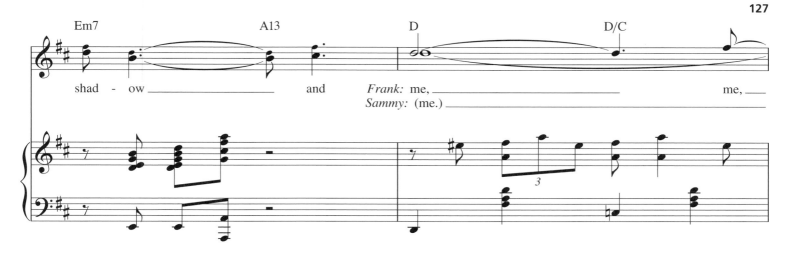

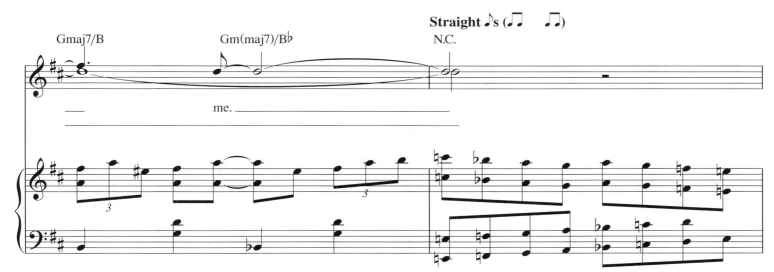

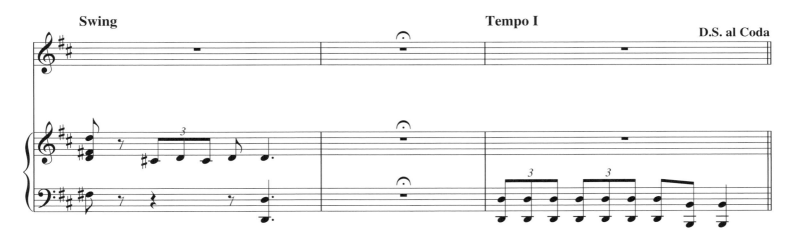

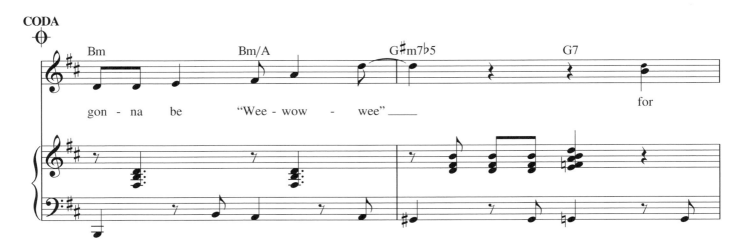

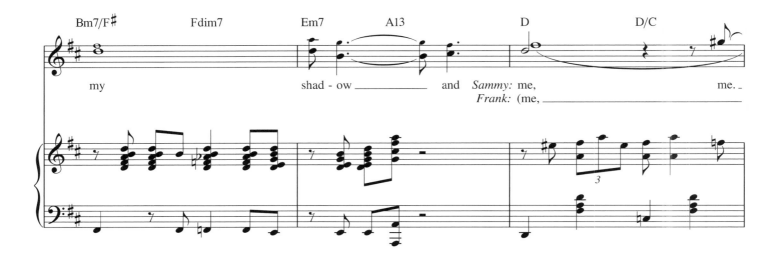

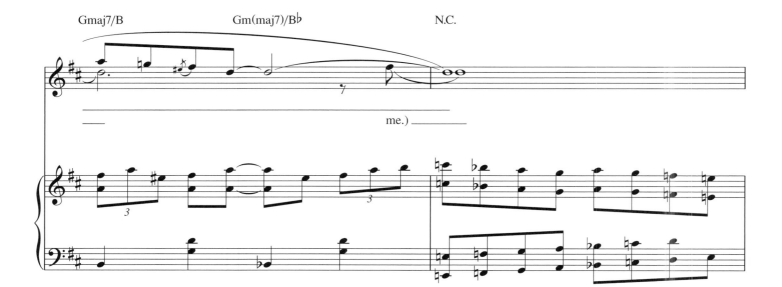

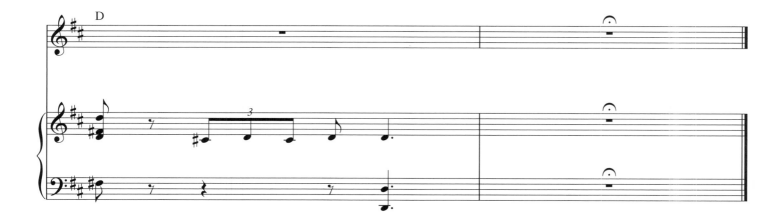